Erotic Fantasy Art

Erotic Fantasy Art

General Editors **ALY FELL & DUDDLEBUG**
Foreword by **JULIE BELL**

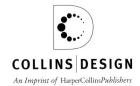

COLLINS|DESIGN
An Imprint of HarperCollins*Publishers*

EROTIC FANTASY ART

HarperCollins books may be purchased for educational,
business, or sales promotional use.
For information, please write:
Special Markets Department, HarperCollins*Publishers*,
10 East 53rd Street, New York, NY 10022.

First published in North America in 2008 by:
Collins Design
An Imprint of HarperCollins*Publishers*
10 East 53rd Street
New York, NY 10022
Tel: (212) 207-7000
Fax: (212) 207-7654
collinsdesign@harpercollins.com
www.harpercollins.com

Distributed throughout North America by:
HarperCollins*Publishers*
10 East 53rd Street
New York, NY 10022
Fax: (212) 207-7654

Library of Congress Control Number: 2007935952
ISBN: 978-0-06-144151-6

Printed in China
Second Printing, 2008

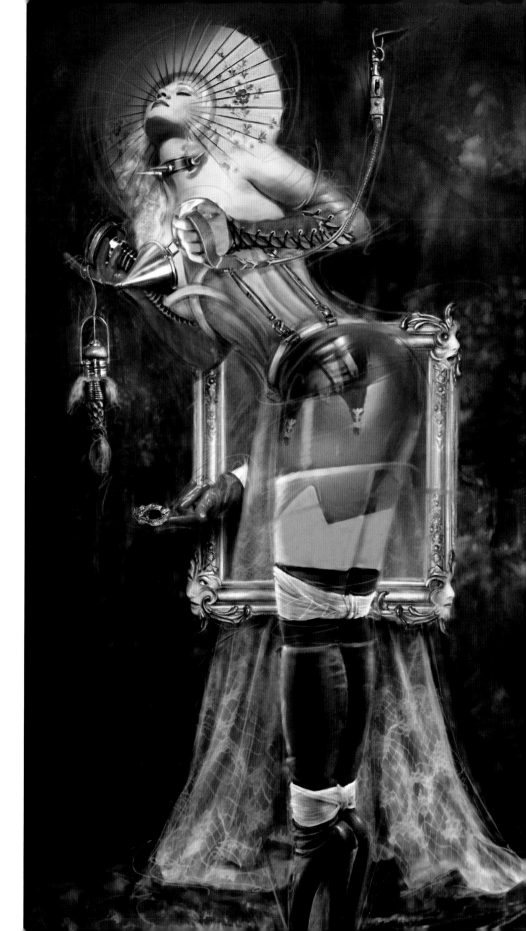

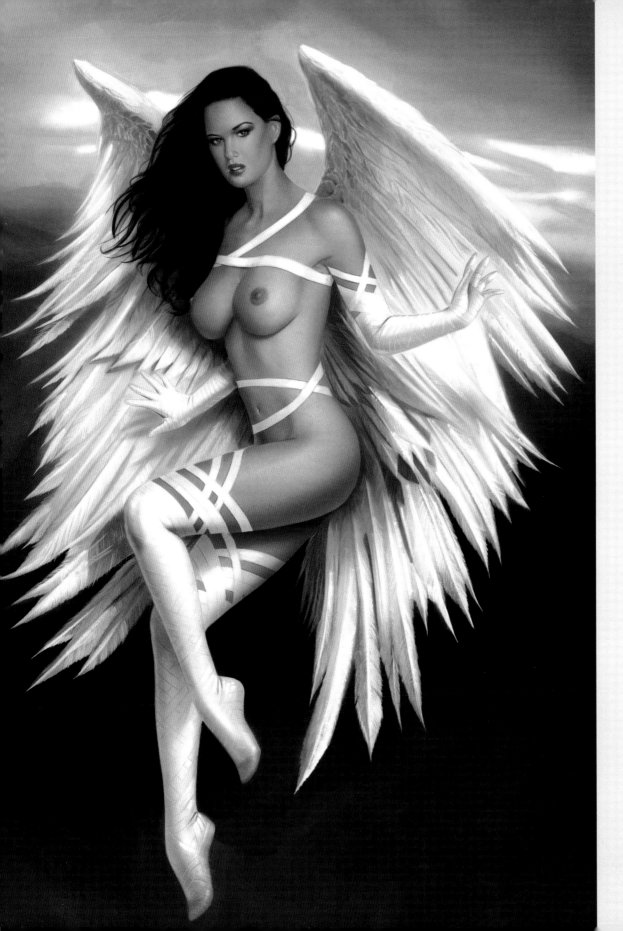

Contents

6 Foreword

8 Introduction

12 Warrior Women and Barbarian Babes

36 Maidens of Honor and Damsels in Distress

68 Wanton Witches and Sexy Sorceresses

96 Femme Fairies and Erotic Elves

130 Dangerous Liaisons with Demonic Dames

154 Futuristic Females and Sci-Fi Foxes

190 Artist Directory

192 Acknowledgments

Thanks to our collective attraction to the beauty and pleasures of the human form, we continue to coexist with our magnificent planet Earth. Our need to express our feelings about this attraction for each other through our art can be so intense that it becomes a form of worship; ancient and touching. Because it is rooted at the very center of our being, it is an art form that speaks with the honesty and purity of DNA itself. And since the raw material for erotic art begins with the never-ending demand of Life to fight for its own existence, to insist on its own continuation, we can't resist looking at it and enjoying it. And why should we resist?

Of course, since the human erotic feeling is so extremely powerful, strong attempts have been made throughout history to make us resist looking and enjoying, to control our natural thoughts and urges. They say control like that is what separates us from the animals. But hold on a second, aren't we part of the animal kingdom, too? And while it's true that such a great power as sexuality needs the balancing force of "great responsibility" to go along with it, many cultures have unfortunately gone so far as to enforce the shackles of shame on the minds of those who would choose to openly indulge in such pleasures.

But maybe the induced shame then becomes a secondary fetish for some? The spicy forbidden can become even more tantalizing, and serves only to add a new layer of excitement to the picture. It's how the stubborn and tenacious human brain works. It is simply hard-wired to enjoy eroticism and—rules and regulations be damned—it's going to enjoy it, shamed or not. It's like the old saying… when life hands you lemons, make lemonade.

Self-adornment, make-up, jewelry, piercings, tattoos—all are expressions of erotic fantasy art. The way we move and use our voices is all part of our beautiful dance of life. We are living, breathing, bumping and grinding works of art. That most fantasy art depicts beautiful people reveling in the glory of their mysterious sensual powers is testament to the fact that we wholeheartedly welcome the effects of the hypnotic drug of eroticism. This is amazing when you consider how often we fiercely resent any force that has so much power over us. But I guess that's where the fantasy part comes in! Raw sexual power, shaped and illustrated through the fantasy of the artist, is then securely contained and controlled in the imagination of the viewer.

I, for one, think that we humans are lovely creatures with a heartbreakingly sweet need to connect with each other. Erotic fantasy art provides a perfect expression of creation and connection that is as deep and true as the explosive birth of a new star, or the soft and silent opening of a flower.

Julie Bell, 2007

Introduction

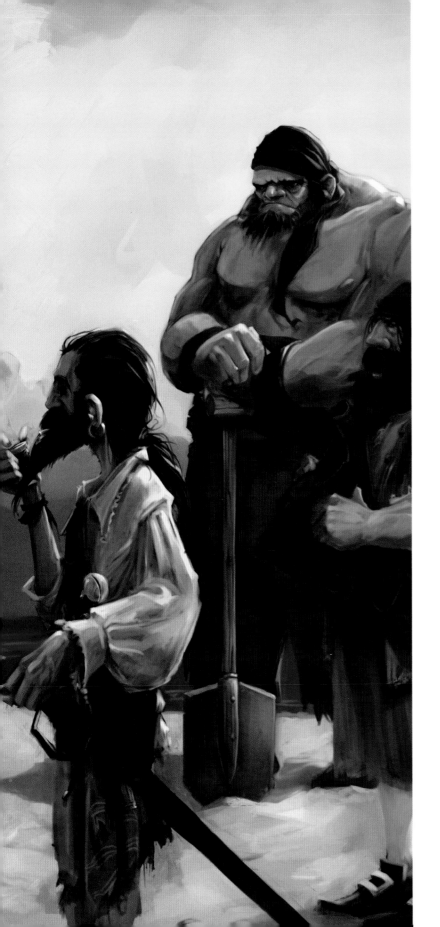

Compiling a collection of erotic fantasy art must be one of the most exciting things an artist can be asked to do. Particularly for those who enjoy creating erotic art themselves. It's like being a kid in a sweetshop!

We are bombarded with sexually oriented imagery all day, every day of our lives, but usually the sexual aspect is secondary to what the image is trying to do. Advertising uses sexually charged imagery to sell us things, and the media uses it to draw us in. Art dedicated to erotic fantasy may have more than one meaning, but there are no hidden agendas; ultimately it aims to excite, stimulate, and thrill us, and to a greater or lesser degree it is self-contained.

Everyone's idea of eroticism is different, and collecting examples together shows how diverse and eclectic the artist's imagination can be. We all have an idea of what fundamentally "turns us on," and the ability of the artist to represent their own idealized vision taps into our fantasies, our stimuli, and creates an opportunity to push the imagination to all sorts of worlds and places where perhaps we might not have ventured alone. One of the parameters we set ourselves with this book was not to shut something out purely because it did not appeal directly to our own imaginations. This collection is not about us, or our individual tastes, but rather an insight into what can be. We wanted it to be an inclusive collection rather than an exclusive one. There are different sexual, cultural and ethnic sensibilities on display here that sometimes have different perspectives. And that is just what we wanted; exploring method, motivation, and technique, from realism and detailed rendering to stylization and graphical styles.

We were also very clear that what we wanted to present here was eroticism and not pornography. There is an age-old argument as to what constitutes both—"one person's meat is another's poison." But ultimately it comes down to imagination. Eroticism hints at possibilities: the fold in the cloth, the weight of hair on a shoulder, or the understated look in the eye under an arched eyebrow. All allow you to escape and exercise your mind's eye. Pornography manipulates you into a state of mind that exploits the trust the viewer has in the artist. It's the difference between driving for yourself and using a chauffeur.

Because this is a collection of erotic art from the fantasy genre, certain themes and patterns emerged as we started to receive artwork from all over the world, and as a result the book can be divided up into distinct chapters. There is every-

thing here, from self-reliant, domineering witch-queens to futuristic, laser-wielding space heroines. From submissive slave girls to mysterious mermaids. All of them contained within the realm of fantasy: that place in the imagination that we are allowed to dip our toe in because it is just that— fantasy, and not reality.

Contained within the pages are artworks from some very well-known and respected artists, who have a long career in fantasy art, not always necessarily from the erotic side of things. What we were able to do was provide them with a platform to do something that maybe their clients wouldn't always ask for; to exercise a little erotic "muscle" so to speak! The results are enlightening and entertaining. Alongside them are less well-known artists—the rising stars who may be seeing their art in a collection for the first time. Some images were created specially for the book, whereas others represent examples from the artists' portfolios and commissions. What results is a collection of enormous energy and imagination that picks up the gauntlet and gives hope for the future of fantasy art. There are book, CD and comic covers, illustrations, concept art and—most of all—personal work, unfettered by the constraints of a brief or an editorial instruction.

The range of technique and medium has expanded quite a bit in recent years; the development of computer processes and various digital painting packages have broadened the artist's repertoire when it comes to presenting their imagination. Alongside digital art there is still—and will always be—the "traditional" approach. Oils, watercolor, pencil and paper, and canvas are healthily, and thankfully, represented here in symbiosis with "pushed pixels." So often, with some of the latest digital processes, it becomes difficult to tell them apart as emulation of traditional technique becomes better in a digital medium. This can be a double-edged sword, but ultimately it can only be for the good. For is it not the final image and motivation that is important, rather than the process used to achieve that vision? It is all too easy to get hung up on medium rather than intent, an intent which here, in *Erotic Fantasy Art*, is healthily apparent. This collection is a melting pot of that very intent, and seeing artwork in print is a hundred times better than flicking past it while browsing the internet. Ink gives a tangibility and validity to something which otherwise can become lost in the digital ether.

The process of bringing all the artwork together was a labor of love for us both. We were given the chance to contact and invite on board some of our greatest inspirations and idols. It was a pleasure to be able to do this, cementing contacts and making new friends. Both Duddlebug and I have day jobs, so this had to be produced in our "spare" time—time which didn't always coincide with other artists' working schedules. As a result, both of us have become expert jugglers, of both time and commitment.

Aly Fell and Duddlebug, 2007

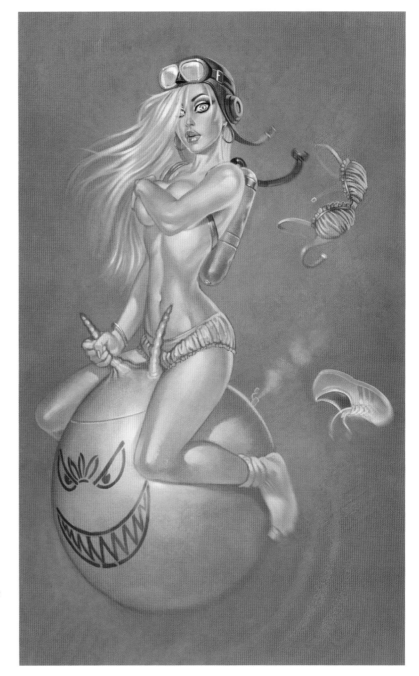

CHAPTER 1

WARRIOR WOMEN AND BARBARIAN BABES

◄ **Radha, Heir to Keld**
Jim Murray
Illustration:
Magic: The Gathering card
Acrylic on watercolor paper
www.jimmurrayart.com

The sketches went back and forth with this one. I didn't really get it at first, but my art director kept pushing me to give her more attitude and make her more of a killer. The end result has a lot more character to it than my early attempts, which goes to show that you should always listen to your art director!

◄ **Messalina**
Alex Horley
Illustration:
Heavy Metal magazine
Acrylic and oil
www.alexhorley.com

The subject was inspired by a historical character; a "dark lady" of the ancient Roman Empire. My goal was to keep a solid classical feel to the painting with just a touch of sci-fi to fit the genre for a Heavy Metal cover. At first I had a regular gladiator in the background, but then decided to change it into a more futuristic warrior to create a more interesting contrast to the classic rendering of the main figure.

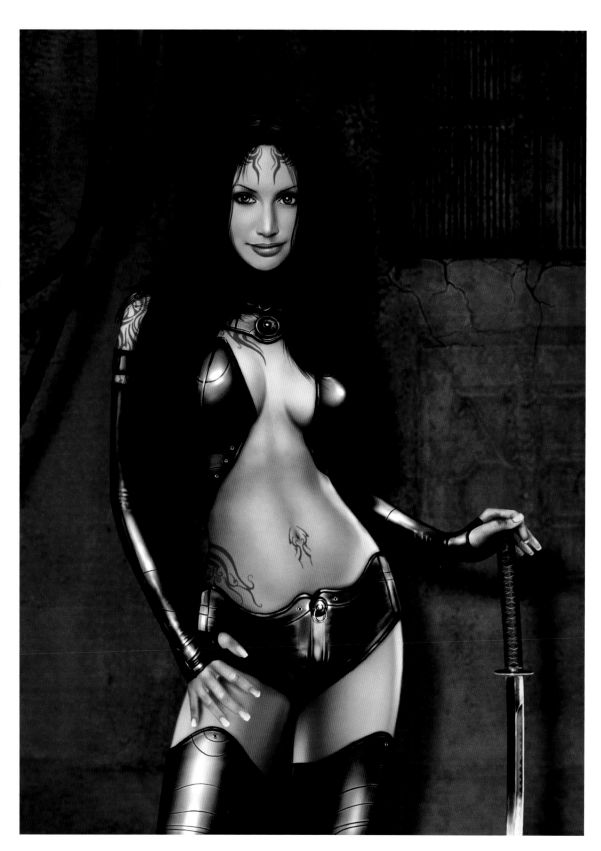

► **Raven**
Tariq Raheem
Portfolio piece
Digital media
www.tariqart.com

In "Raven", Tariq presents us with a bold portrait of a confident and alluring woman whose smile reveals a calm character. A warrior, relaxing with her sword, prior to battle or after? The simple background is typical of portraiture and draws our focus on the girl and her violet eyes.

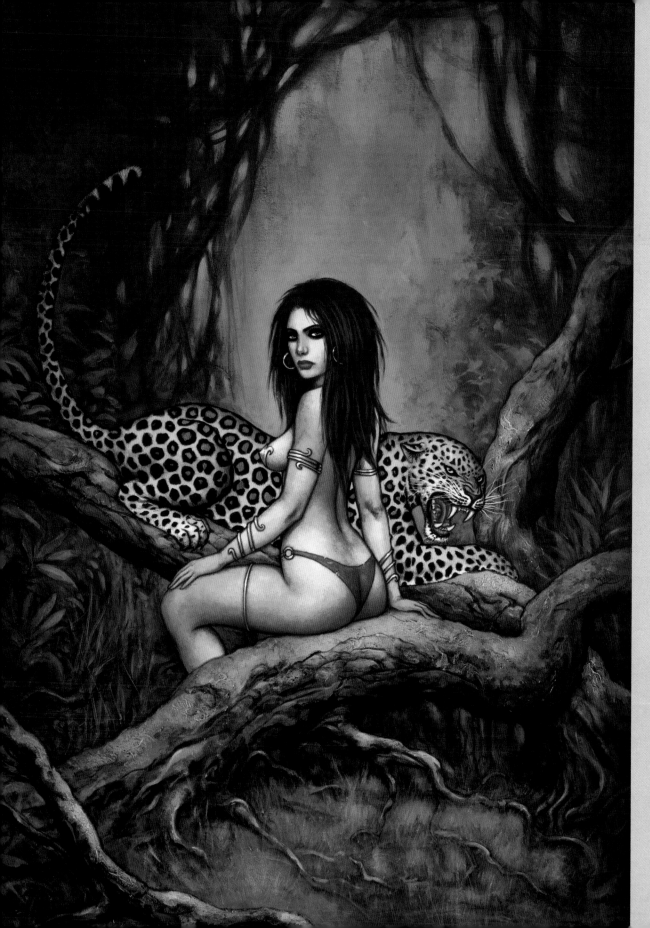

◄ **Leopard Girl**
Scott Lewis
Portfolio piece
Acrylic on board
www.lewisart.com

This personal piece from Scott was an indulgence in his favourite subject matter. "Girls and big cats—my favorite subjects and great material for a painting." Even without the fangs and the snarl, this jungle girl stares as defiantly from the canvas as her leopard.

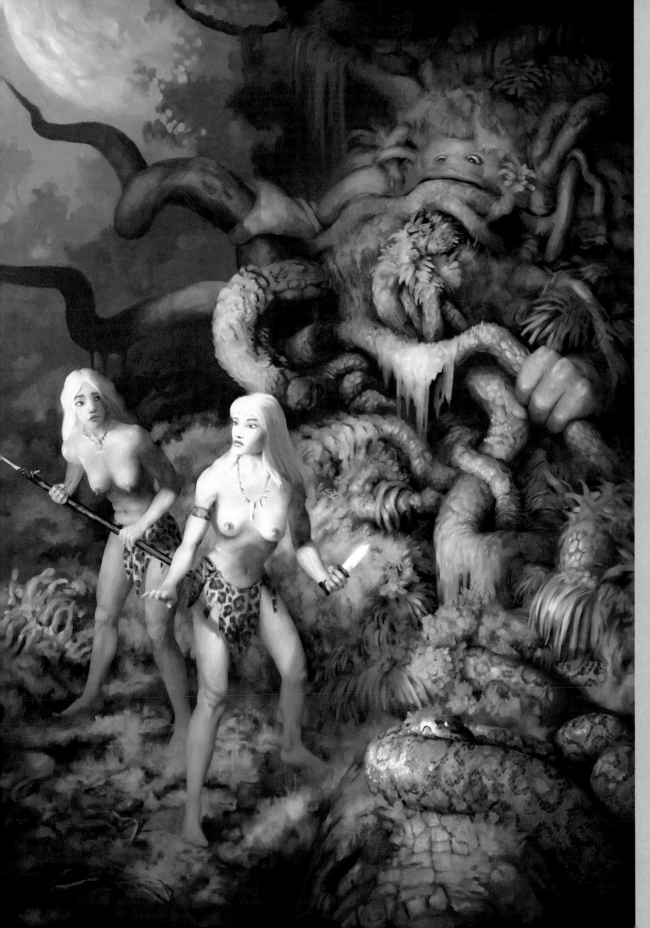

◀ **The Green Man**
Simon Dominic Brewer
Portfolio piece
Corel Painter

*In this piece I wanted to create
something lighthearted, but at
the same time a bit spooky. We
can see the green man hidden
in the foliage, but we don't yet
know whether he's friend or
foe. Will he rescue the warrior
women from the snake, or add
to their troubles?*

◀◀ **0 Abate (The Slaughter)**
Steve Sampson
Portfolio piece
Adobe Photoshop and Illustrator
www.sampsonart.com

With this image I decided to illustrate the characters with vectors, just using Photoshop to add a few finishing touches.

▶ **Broken World**
R.K Post
Commission: Gaspowered Games
Digital media
www.rkpost.net

A video game cover with the core iconic character of the Dungeon Siege franchise breaking apart the world with little struggle at all. I want to thank Marcie for giving me the opportunity, and fighting for the original vision.

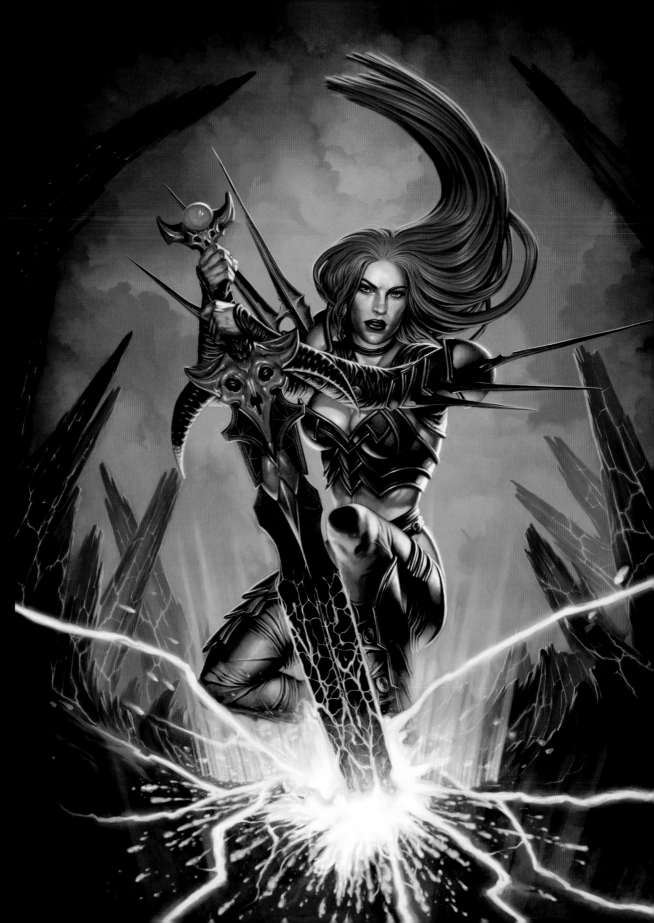

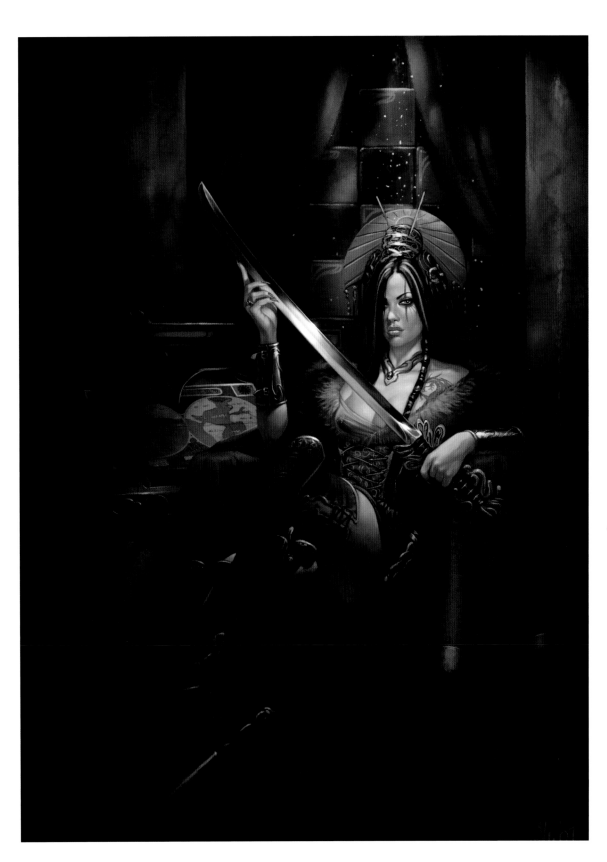

◀ **The Black Queen**
Aly Fell
Portfolio piece
Adobe Photoshop
www.darkrising.co.uk

Originally produced for an online art challenge, I came back to this to alter a few things that I was never comfortable with. Sometimes, returning to an image isn't a good idea, but in this case I was never happy with the original face and felt a revision was called for. Inspired by elements of Asian dress and mixed with a dose of art nouveau, The Black Queen sits on her throne, arrogant and dispassionate. Her distaste for the artist painting her portrait is all too apparent.

▶ **The Dragon Princess**
Svetlin Velinov
Client: Future Publishing
Adobe Photoshop
www.velinov.com

Svetlin wanted to portray a contradiction in this image; a battle of elements and feelings that were all subservient to the heroine's will. The powerful reds and oranges help to present this idea, but this is no subservient protagonist — she is truly master of her universe.

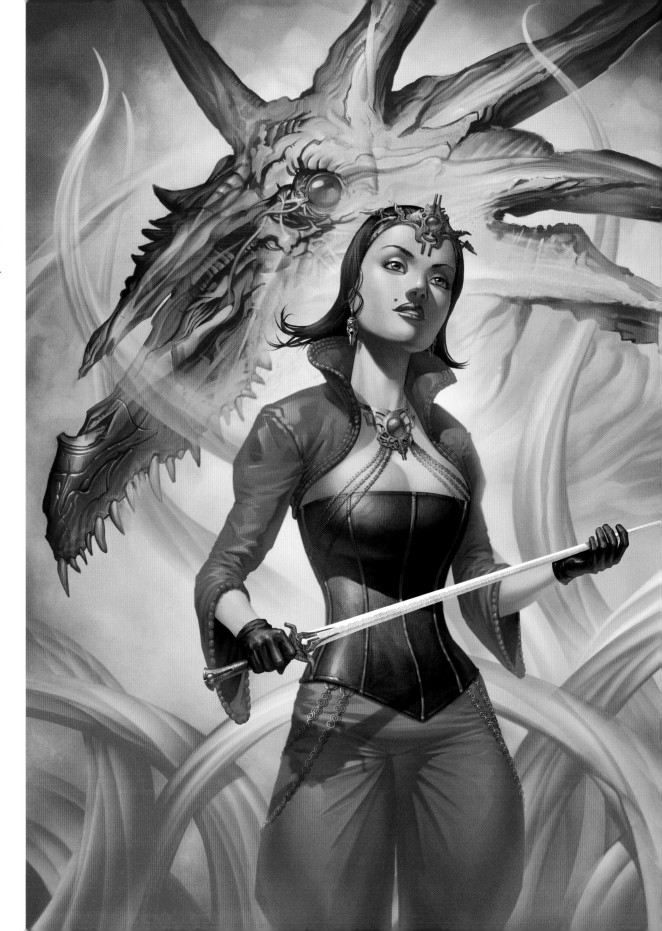

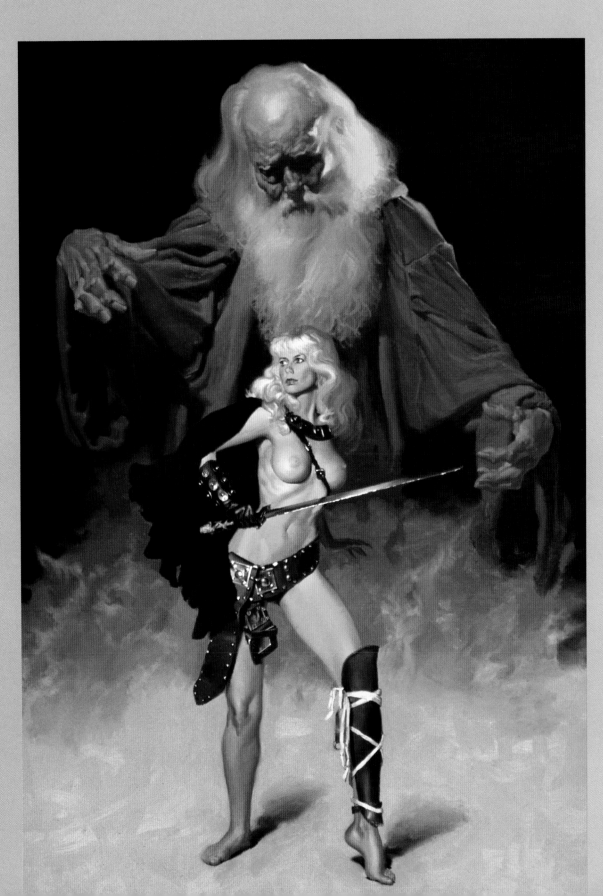

► **Wizard's Champion**
Glen Orbik
Portfolio piece
Oil
www.orbikart.com

This started out as a sample piece. As minimal as this costume is, the heavy leather pieces and cape kept sliding around on our model during the shoot. We realized how impractical for a warrior this would be—but who cares? She looked great (and we all took turns playing with the sword afterward). This piece hung at the art school where I teach. One night, someone broke in and stole several paintings. I'm not sure if I felt more relief or the ultimate critique that they didn't steal mine too!

24

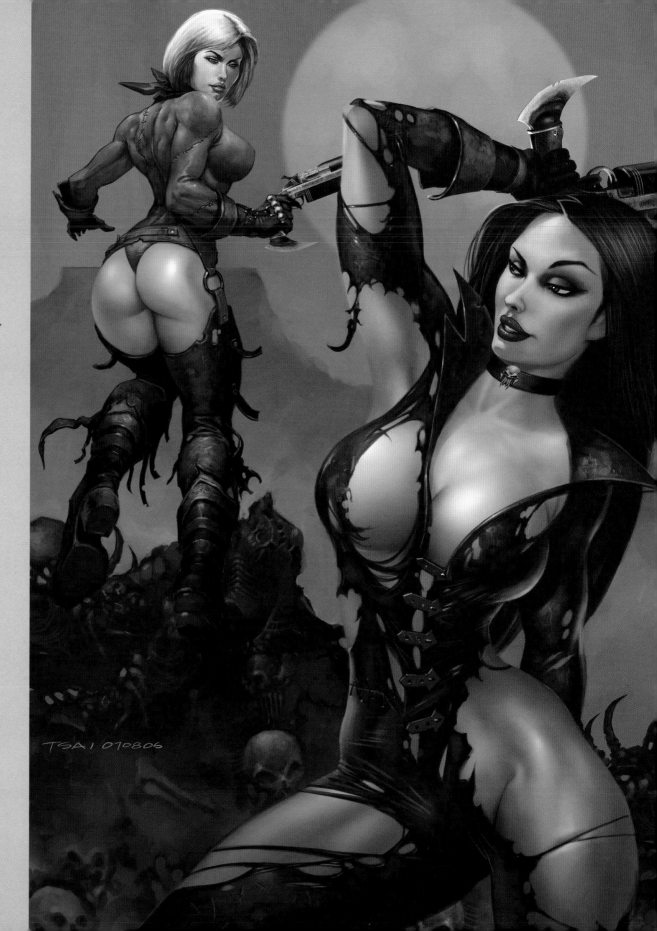

► **Duel**

Francis Tsai
Commission: High Moon/Vivendi
Digital media
www.teamgt.com

*This painting was for the
"Darkwatch" video game from
High Moon/Vivendi. It was
originally commissioned as part
of a character trading card
special for Playboy magazine.
The trading cards had portions
of the image printed on the back,
so if you collected all the cards
they could be assembled to form
the full picture.*

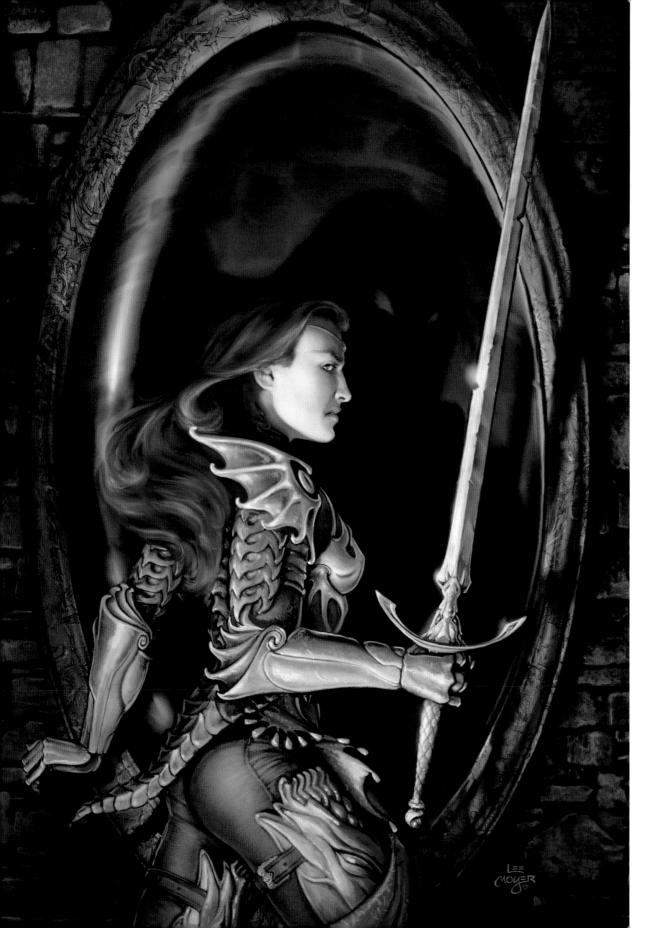

◄ **The Ebon Mirror**
Lee Moyer
Book cover: *The Ebon Mirror*
by Keith Baker
Mixed media: Pencil, Acrylic,
Bryce, Adobe Photoshop
www.leemoyer.com

*Before Keith Baker created
"Eberron" (the newest Dungeons
& Dragons universe) I had the
great pleasure of illustrating
his first published book. The
cover shows a most remarkable
Paladin coming to grips with the
Vampiric horror that awaits her
on the other side of the mirror.
Though originally painted in
acrylic, I have since modified it
several times on the computer
and every revision brings it
closer to my original vision.
I'm not yet convinced that
the piece is finished...*

熊猫小姐
第一個美籍亞洲人的女超級英雄
清水裕子画

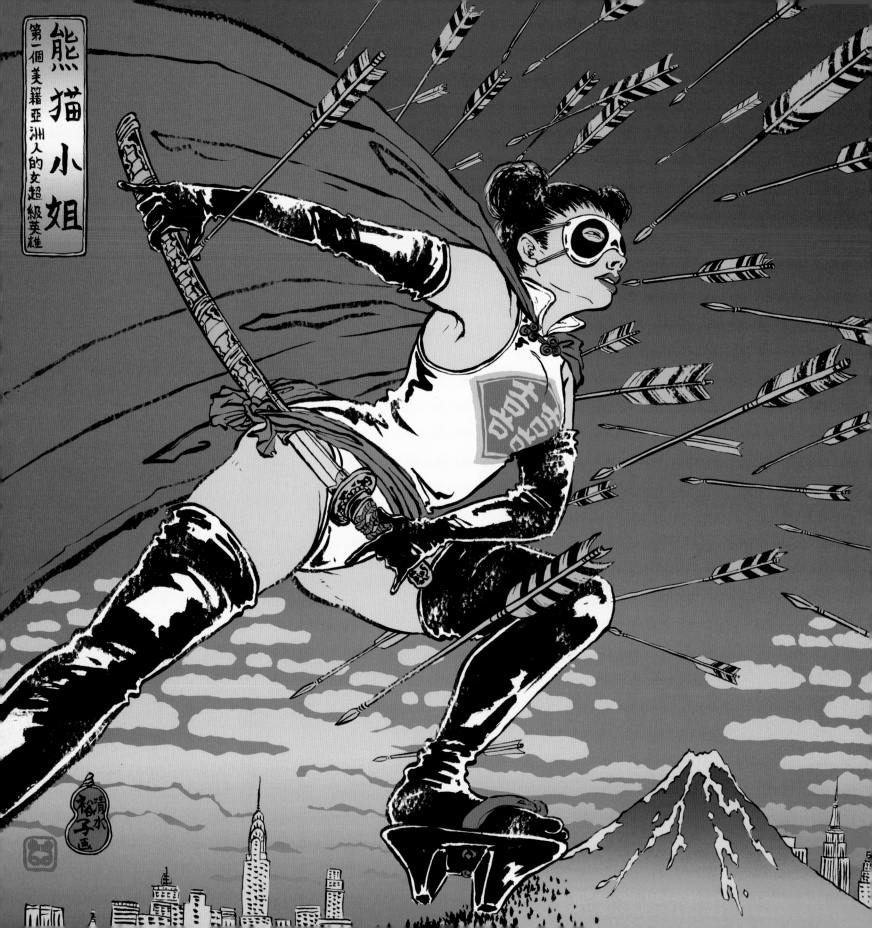

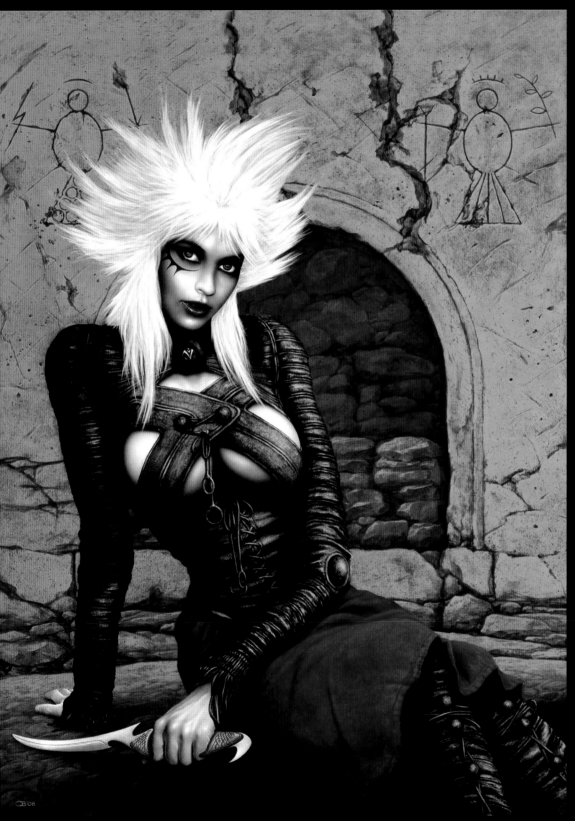

◄◄ **Panda Girl: The First Asian-American Superheroine**
Yuko Shimizu
Client: Murphy Design (USA)
Ink drawing and Adobe Photoshop
www.yukoart.com

Panda Girl was featured in the "Artistic Utopia" calendar by Murphy Design, and depicts an Asian-inspired superheroine flying into a barrage of arrows. She has the standard red cape of the American superhero, but draws a Japanese katana in her defence. There is an erotic tinge to her costume with the shiny black stockings and gloves. In the background a Fuji-esque mountain merges with a New York skyline.

◄ **Sirpa of the Guild of Vammatar**
Jim Burns
Cover: *Heavy Metal* magazine
Acrylic
www.jimburns.co.uk

Heavy Metal magazine essentially gave me a free brief for this painting. Bearing in mind the usual approach to their magazine covers—that of feisty, sexy, fantasy/sci-fi females—this was the character that materialized. As I tried to come up with an appropriate name for her, it struck me that she reminded me of some Finnish Goth girls I once saw at a convention. Consequently, I gave her the Finnish name "Sirpa" (found by accident in a cookery book!) and decided to connect her to an imaginary guild, although the myth of Vammatar—a goddess of pain and suffering—does exist!

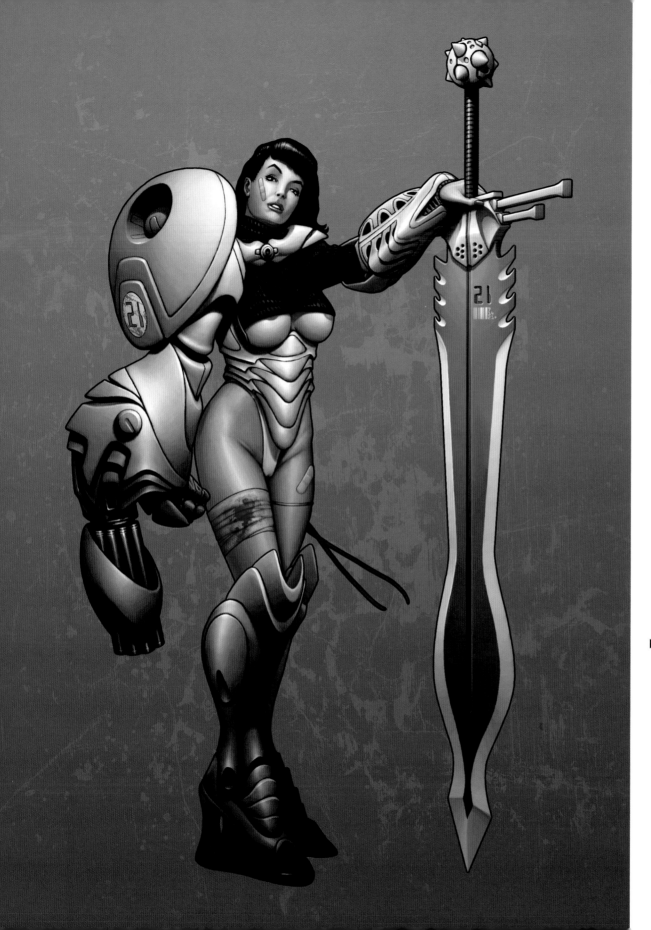

◄ **Blackjack Betty**
Malachai Maloney (Liquidwerx)
Portfolio piece
Digital media
www.liquidwerx.com

Blackjack Betty is the culmination of my love of pin-up, fantasy, and sci-fi art. She is a femme fatale in the truest sense; both beautiful and deadly. The original Blackjack Betty design was done in 2004 and has subsequently led to numerous other Blackjack Betty incarnations, paintings, concept designs, and now a graphic novel. When I was creating this character my thoughts behind her were simple; I wanted her to appeal to male audiences for obvious reasons — her sexuality and good looks — while still appealing to female audiences because of her intelligence, strength, and bravery.

► **MG42 Madchen**
Andrew Bawidamann
Personal piece
Mixed media/digital
www.bawidamann.com

Andrew enjoys military pin-ups, and his strong graphic style gives him ample opportunity to present these appealing sexy images in a classic pin-up way. Using the bullet belt to frame the character is a clever device in this strongly designed piece from Andrew. The color palette is simple and direct, and befits the military theme.

©BAWIDAMANN

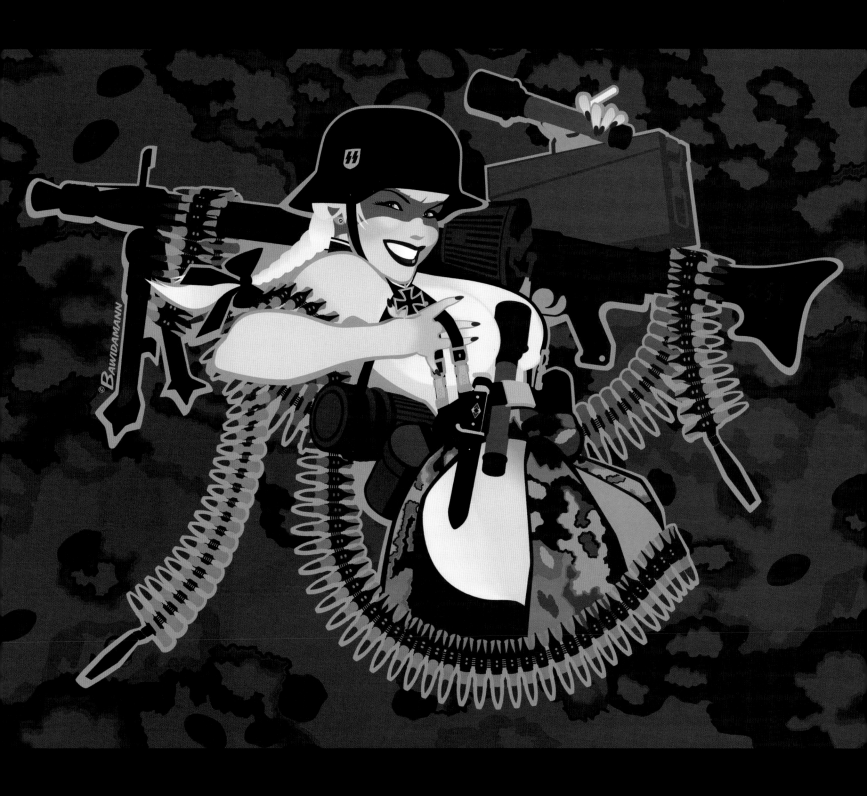

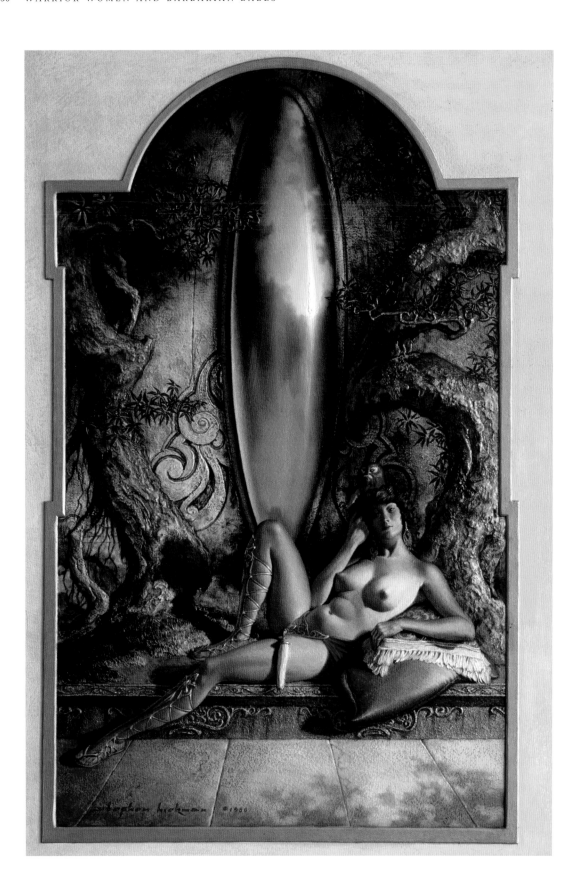

◄ **Lemurian Princess**
Stephen Hickman
Private commission
Oils
www.stephenhickman.com

Stephen Hickman wrote his novel "The Lemurian Stone" in 1988, and has produced a series of paintings that have expand his visual interpretation of this world and its people. In this painting, the Lemurian princess reclines on cushions before the Lemurian Stone; a portal to other worlds.

▶ **Rebecca Fantasy**
Tariq Raheem
Portfolio piece
Digital media
www.tariqart.com

Another character portrait with a warrior woman as the theme. The detail here is reserved for the amazingly rendered metalwork of the armor, and the bold tattoos. From the pointed ears it would appear that Rebecca is probably a warrior "elf."

32

► **Asylum of Horrors**
Ben Olson
Client: Asylum Press,
Art direction: Frank Forte
Digital media
www.sketchthing.com

This illustration is for "Asylum of Horrors"—a collected volume of comic book horror stories. The only direction I received was to paint a twisted creature and add some T&A. I have a handful of themes that I fall back on when I don't know what else to do. Torturing small animals is usually a hit, so I came up with the idea of a scantily clad girl eating cats with a weird cat monster hovering in the background. The cats turned into skinned cat mutants because I thought they would be more fun to paint.

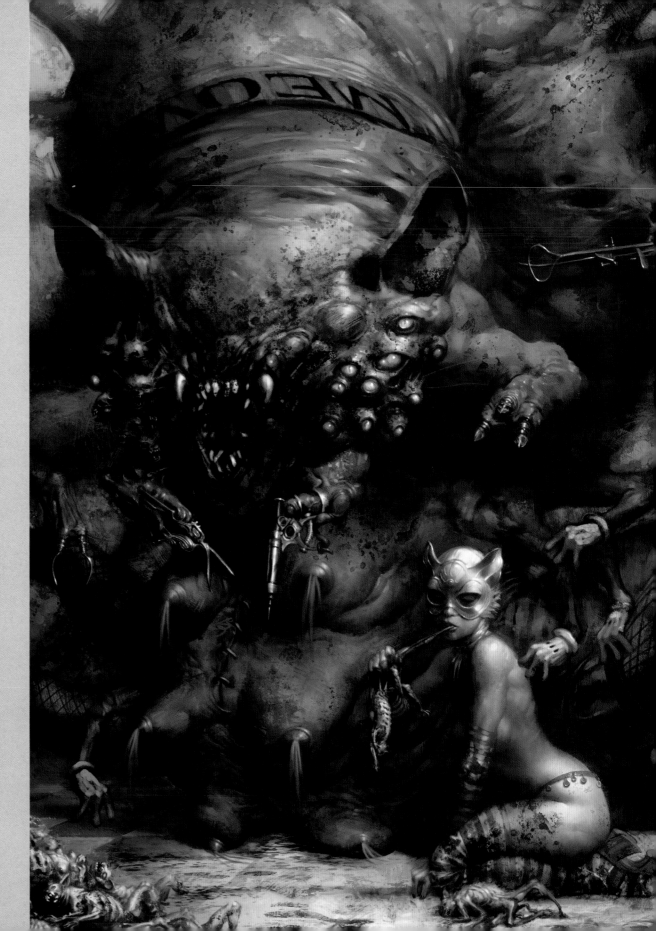

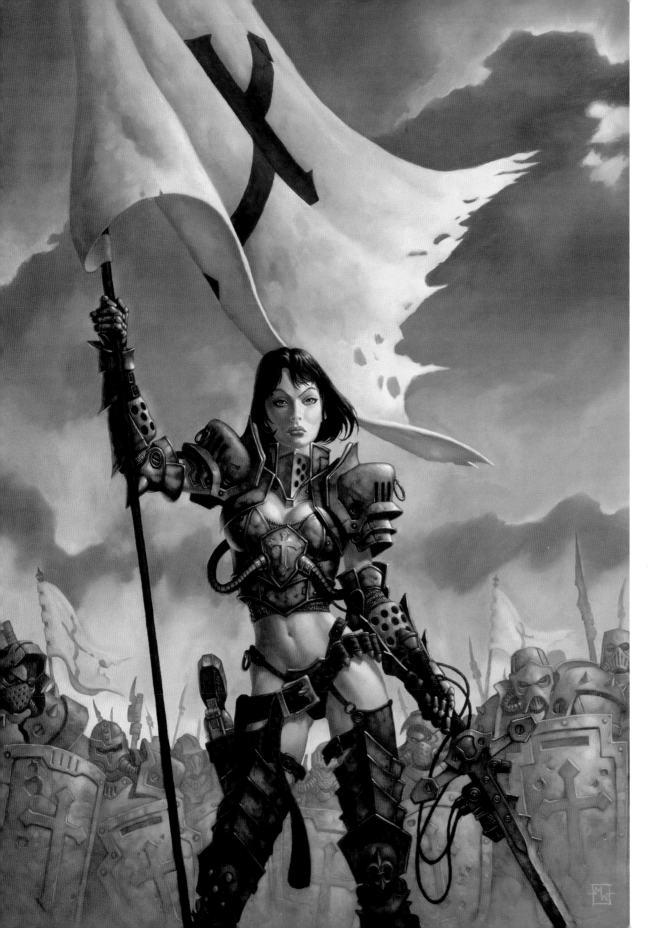

◀ **Cross**
Matt Wilson
Illustration:
Heavy Metal magazine
Oil on board-mounted paper
www.mattwilsonart.com

*"Cross" was originally created
as a cover for Heavy Metal
magazine. It was a blue-sky
project and I had the great
opportunity to work with Kevin
Eastman as the art director.
Unfortunately, a couple of
months before it was meant to
see print, the editor changed
their format and only wanted to
feature artwork by a few well-
known pin-up artists. This image
was relegated to an artist-bio
spread and hasn't ever seen print
anywhere else until now.*

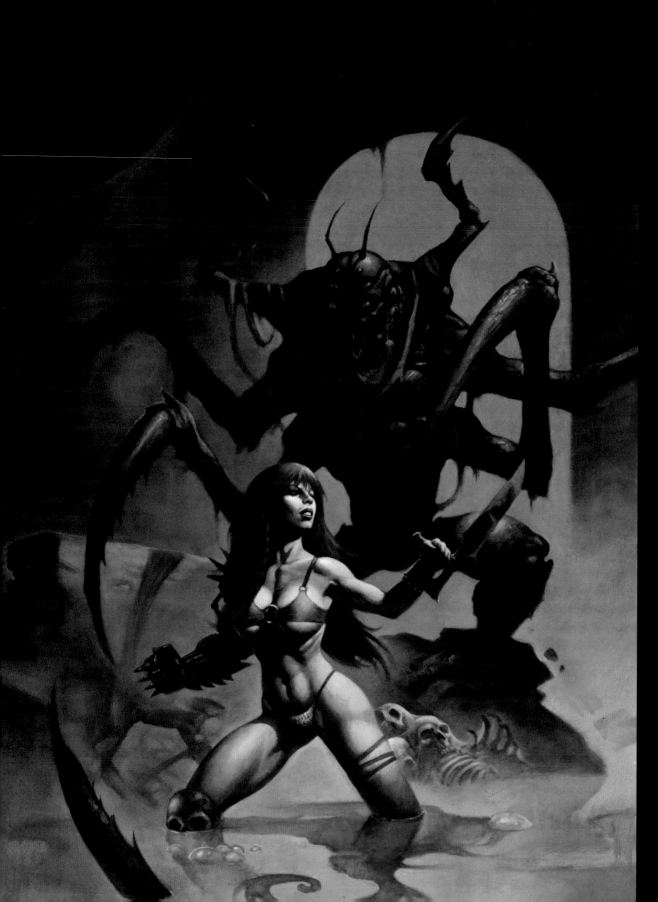

Maxine
Alex Horley
Portfolio piece
Acrylic and oil
www.alexhorley.com

This painting is one of the rare occasions where I got to paint what I want. The main character is from a comic book mini-series I worked on called "Sharky", where she was supposed to be the rejected daughter of Odin. In a short story that appeared in Heavy Metal a few years ago, she and Sharky fight together against a giant bug. This painting refers to that story, with an updated look for the character, as well as the monster. This was to be the cover for a trade paperback, collecting the entire series, as well as that short story. Unfortunately, the book was never published and the painting did not get used.

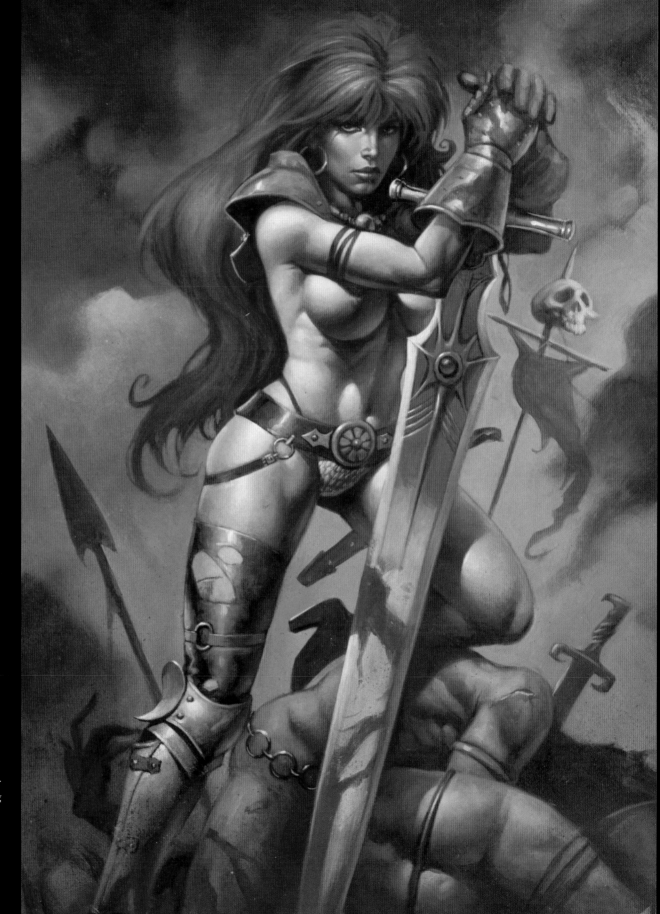

► **Red Stacy**
Alex Horley
Portfolio piece
Acrylic and oil
www.alexhorley.com

This is the first painting I did of Stacy E. Walker, so it is very special to me (us). After meeting her in person, I really wanted to transfer my impression of her true personality into the warrior girl in the painting, not just her image. The character has just ended a fierce battle with her impossibly big sword, suggesting empowerment, yet her eyes give us a feeling of inner vulnerability—a very interesting contrast I found intriguing and unique to Stacy. She would go on to become the biggest inspiration to my work and my life in general.

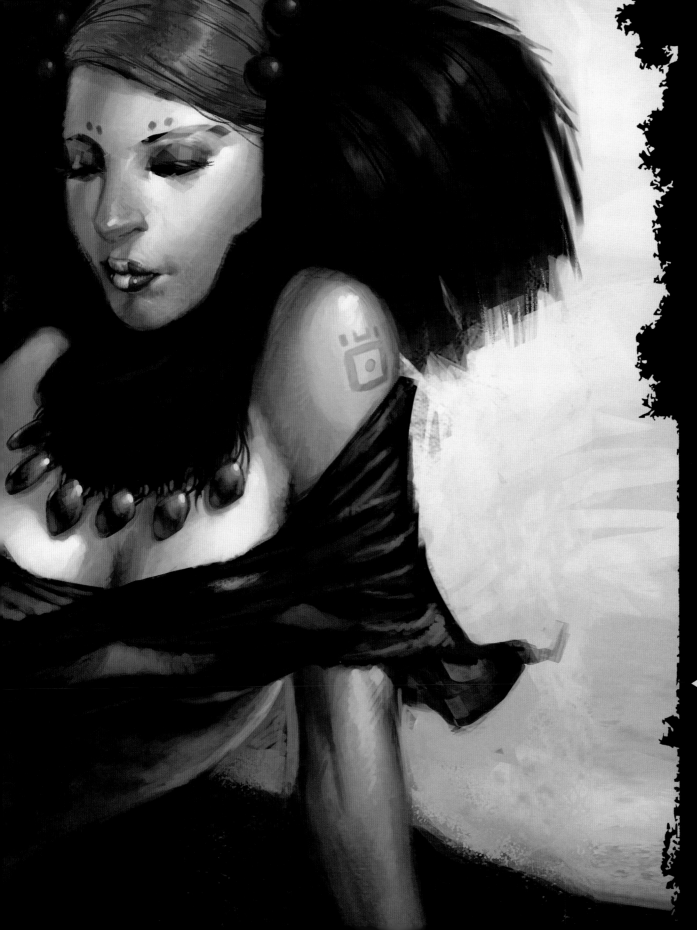

CHAPTER 2
MAIDENS OF HONOR AND DAMSELS IN DISTRESS

◄ **Chloe**
Izzy Medrano
Portfolio piece
Adobe Photoshop
www.mercilessdesign.com

This serene portrait of a relaxed girl, beautifully rendered with simple brush marks is, Izzy tells us, "A life painting, straight from my noggin". The strong lighting and tattoos make this apparently normal image seem otherworldly.

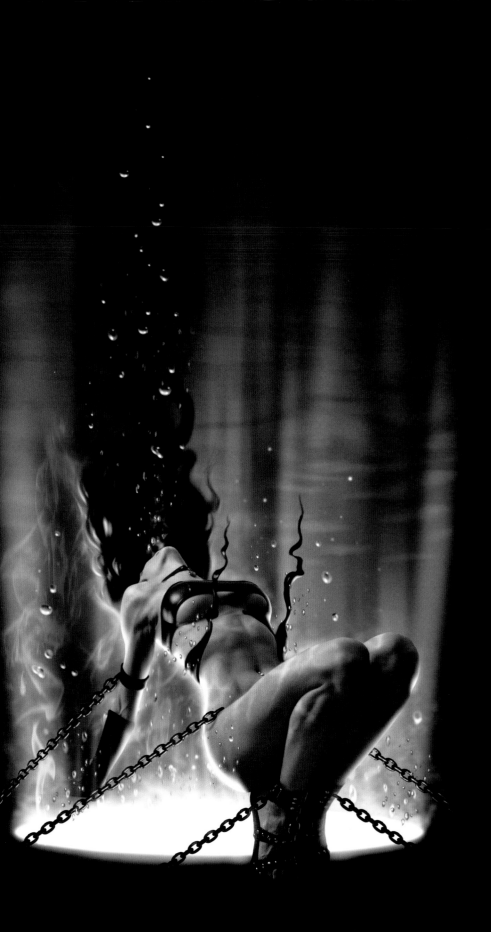

◄ **The Tank**
Tony Mauro
Portfolio piece
Adobe Photoshop
www.darkdayproductions.com

*This piece was originally
titled "Not all of the witches
were burned at the stake." I'm
especially fond of this piece
because of the reaction it gets
from people when they see it.
I've got such a wide range of
emotions out of people that it has
really taken on a life of its own.
I like how calm and in control
she looks, in spite of the situation
she is in. The model in this piece
is Angela Taylor. She was truly
awesome to work with and has
such a strong camera presence
it's amazing.*

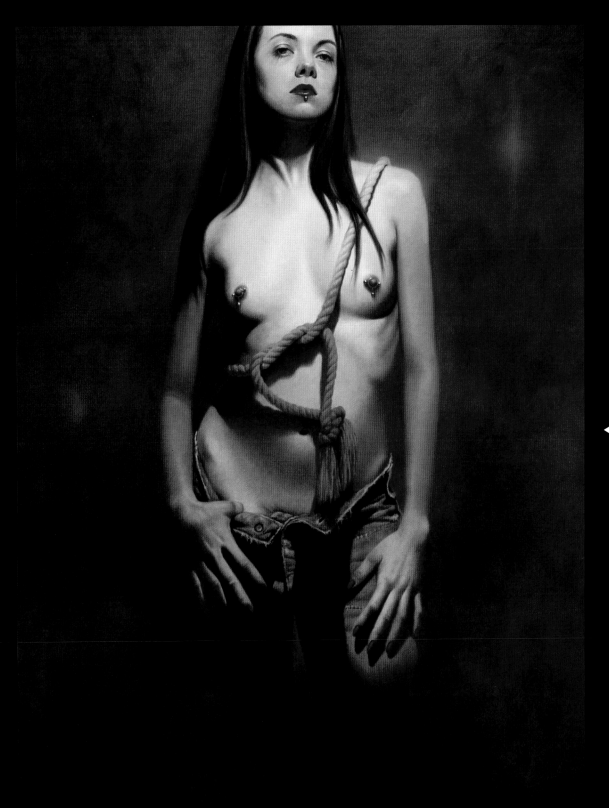

◀ **Raven**
Vince Natale
Book cover: *Lake Mountain*
from Bloodletting Press
Oil
www.vincenatale.com

This is the cover for a limited
edition, collector's version of
a horror/psychological thriller
book entitled Lake Mountain, by
Steve Gerlach. Raven is the prime
character of this book. She's
a six-foot tall "exotic dancer"
at a "gentleman's club" called
Rawhide. She takes an unruly
regular client home to her trailer
and ends up killing him. That's
when the dark adventure begins
for Raven and her girlfriend/
room-mate. My mission was to
come up with a visual character
that expressed the attitude of the
written one in the book – both
appealing and dangerous. A
degree of mystery was also
needed to reflect the tone of
the book.

► **Golden Dragon**

Ric Frane
Portfolio piece
Watercolor
www.ricfrane.com

I do a lot of pin-ups and I love Asian culture. I had this great photo of Linda Tran. I loved the pose and the way she looked, but it just needed a background. I like using traditional themes with pin-ups, so the dragon worked out well. It's one of my favorite paintings.

►► **Sea of Vaynu**

Stephen Hickman
Private commission
Oil
www.stephenhickman.com

In this painting, Stephen Hickman presents us with a princess — naked but for her ornate jewellery and headdress — listening to the strings of her musician. Beyond the princess lies the Sea of Vaynu and a gleaming golden palace. Stephen works in oils, and his paintings have a sense of wonder and beauty that draw on classical architecture and epic landscapes.

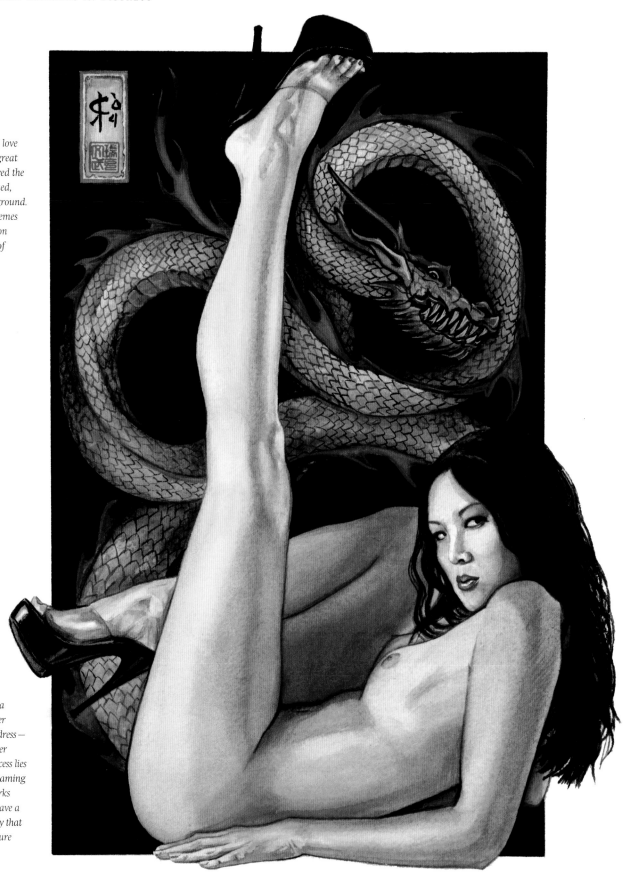

▶ **Devotional Aspiration**
Alan Daniels
Portfolio piece
Acrylics, chalk, oil, and gold leaf
on canvas
www.heavenlyhusseys.com
www.fetish-pinups.com

*"Devotional Aspiration" is the
central figure in a triptych that
gives a new look to the Saints
and Martyrs — the other two
being "Devotional Subjugation"
and "Devotional Supplication".
The feet make this painting!*

▶▶ **Ivy**
Lorenzo Sperlonga
Portfolio piece
Acrylic
www.lorenzosperlonga.com

*In "Ivy", we're not sure whether
the title refers to the girl or the
leaves meandering up the trellis.
However, she is still wonderfully
sexy and presented in a color
palette that is simple and direct.*

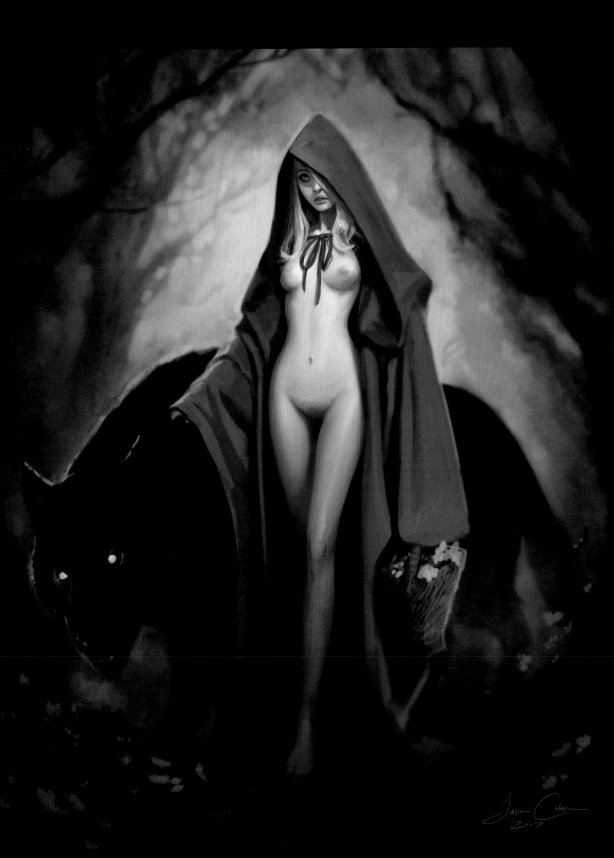

◀ **The Wax-dragon**
Natascha Roeoesli
Portfolio piece
Adobe Photoshop
www.tascha.ch

*I had this background story about
the Wax-dragon in my head for
quite a long time. To be honest I
can't really remember how I came
up with it, but I wanted to bring
the idea to paper. It was definitely
a personal challenge because,
until then, I had never really tried
to paint a dragon, yet this one
had to be quite unique. The wax
effect on the dragon proved to
be particularly tricky, but with
the help of some layer modes I
managed to create the somewhat
realistic effect I was looking for.
The woman as counterpart had
to look mysterious and appealing
at the same time.*

 Red Riding Hood
Jason Chan
Portfolio piece
Digital media
www.jasonchanart.com

*It seems Red has found a way
to pacify the big, bad wolf!
This was basically just a doodle
painting of Red Riding Hood
that kept on developing (no
pun intended.)*

◀ **Ssss...**
Ric Frane
Portfolio piece
Watercolor
www.ricfrane.com

Most of the time I shoot photos with an idea of what I want to paint. I was doing a photo shoot with model Nikki Fritz and my wife, Wendy M, when we came up with this great pose. I didn't know what I was going to do with it, but after a while the picture spoke for itself. They were entwined like snakes, so I added the tails and tried to keep it a little vague. Are they with snakes, or are they part snake?

▶ **Bode Babe**
Mark E. Rogers
Portfolio piece
Acrylic, Adobe Photoshop
www.merogers.com

This is a picture of my friend Lena. She's not the same physical type as most pin-up models, but I think she's pretty sexy — rather like a real-life Vaughn Bode woman. I did four paintings of her, and this was the first. I wasn't expecting it to sell, but it turns out that folks have pretty much the same reaction to Lena as I do.

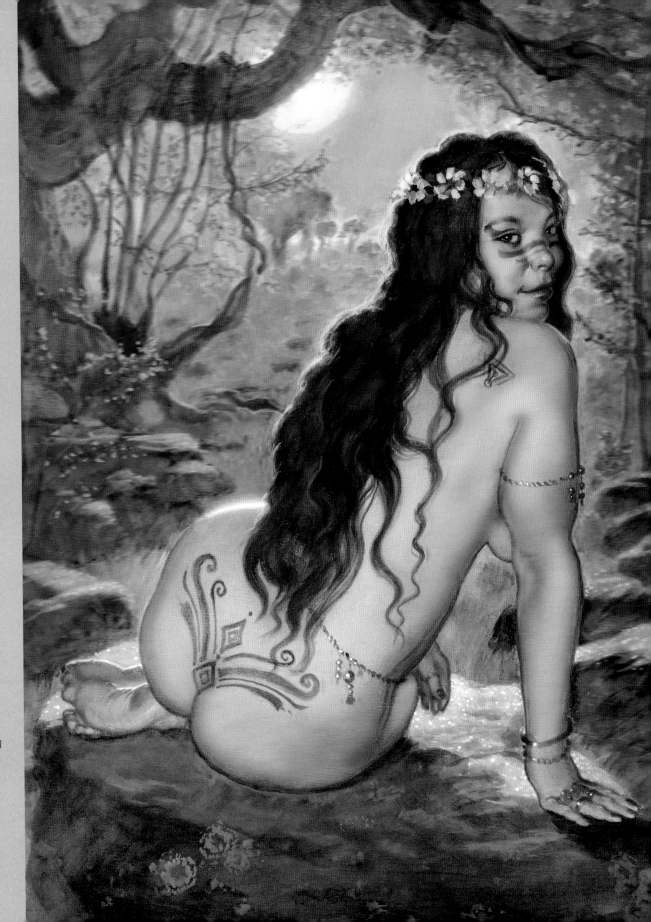

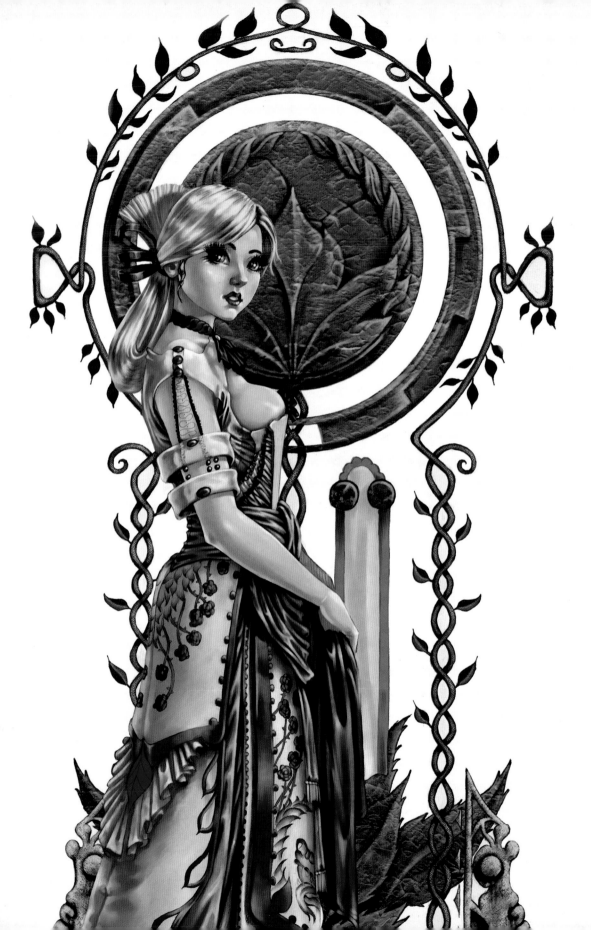

◀ **Elsine**
Andy Hepworth
Portfolio piece
Painter IX.5
www.andyhepworth.com

I don't often combine iconic design with characters in simple ways like this, but this was a study in Asian-inspired Tudor-esque dress, and what better mannequin than a pretty girl? I've always been a sucker for drapery and layers, and like to add a bit of corsetry for good measure.

▶ **AG Thought**
Mark Nelson
Portfolio piece
Pencil and Adobe Photoshop
gdpmark@chorus.net

Mark's composition incorporates intricately detailed pattern with strong emblems and figures. In this piece, the woman faces the fanged skull, whilst the tissues and sinews of her arm spew into the skull and bones in the lower half of the painting. But what the viewer may perceive as sinister, Mark describes differently: "Bones and skulls are not images of death for me, but the beautiful under-structure of life."

► **Masquerade**
Patrick J Jones
Private commission
Oil and Corel Painter
www.pjartworks.com

*This painting was a frontispiece
for the classic horror story, "The
Phantom of the Opera". I've
tinkered with the dress, unlacing
the bodice to suggest the kind
of eroticism that would have
been incongruous if introduced
in a classic novel. The hardest
part of the creative process for
me comes after sketching and
before painting: working out the
lighting, color and atmosphere.
The actual painting, which for
years was the toughest part, is
now the easiest stage.*

►► **Toy**
Zhuzhu
Portfolio piece
Adobe Photoshop
http://zhuzhu.deviantart.com
www.artwanted.com/zhuzhu

*This was a quick idea from
2003, reworked after more
anatomy practice. The
inspiration for this work is
a macabre story. Sometimes
humans are weak, as though
someone controls everything
from the dark.*

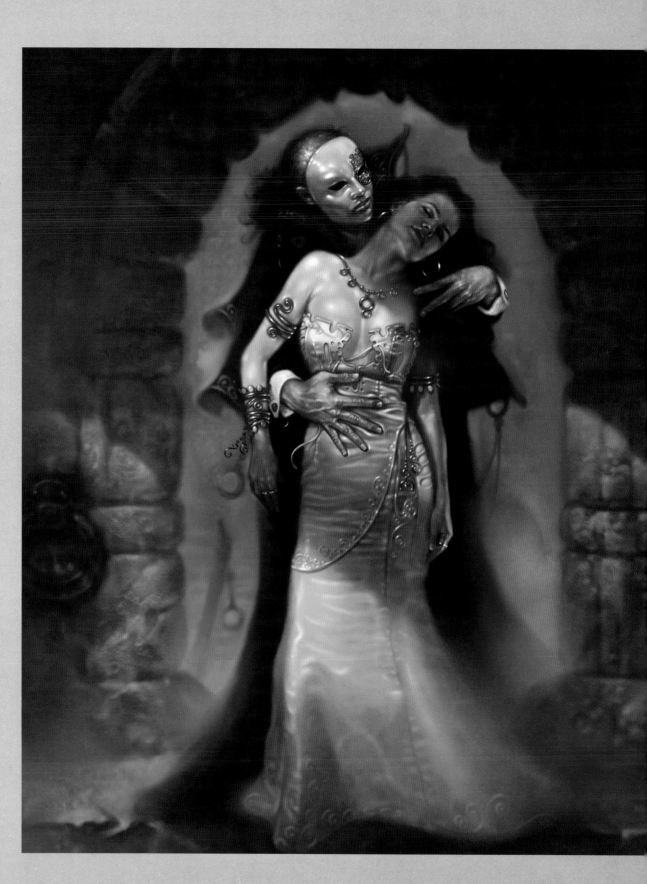

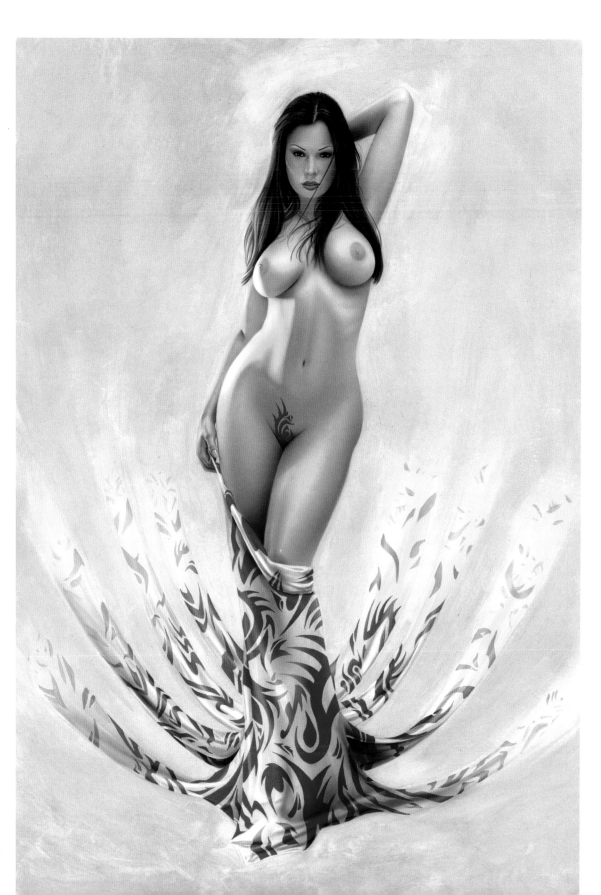

Silk Blossom
Lorenzo Sperlonga
Portfolio piece
Acrylic
www.lorenzosperlonga.com

The beautiful skin tones that
Lorenzo has obviously spent
so much time perfecting on
"Silk Blossom" give a sense of
tangibility to this coy beauty.
The cheekiness of the tattoo is
a lovely touch.

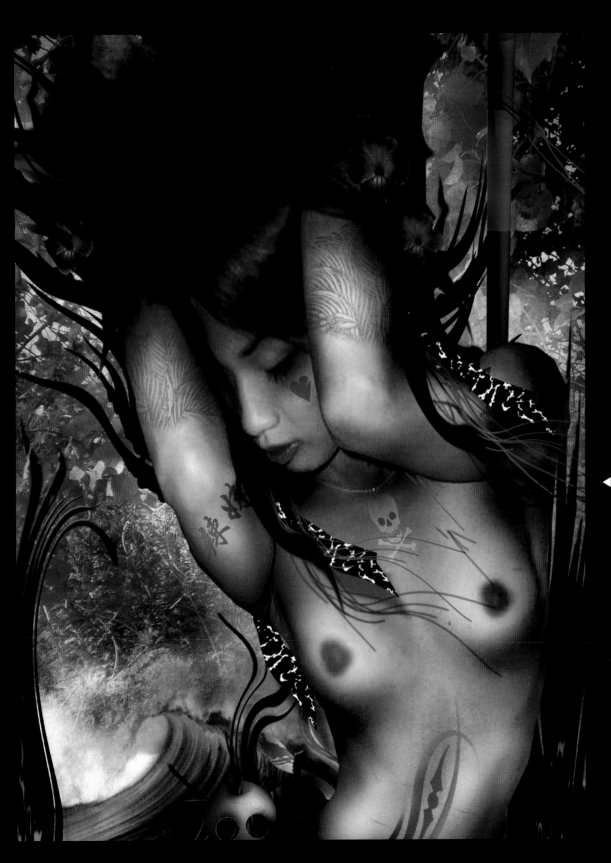

Beach Girl
Chris Spollen
Book illustration: *Surf Beach*
Digital media
www.spollen.com

This piece is from my yet-to-be-published art book entitled **Surf Beach**. *It's based on a small island in the pacific (just south of Krakatoa) that exists in a parallel universe. The islanders pride themselves on recycling, and live in simple hand-painted bungalows. They fashion their clothing from found objects and beads, and create hot-rods— long, low, and loud—from found and reworked engine parts. The women are all of Chinese decent and are quite beautiful. Life is good here and they all live in harmony with nature, except for Saturday night: Race Night!*

▶ **The Chalice**
Aly Fell
Portfolio piece
Adobe Photoshop
www.darkrising.co.uk

*"She presses her forefinger to
her lips and Harpocrates 'hears'
her silent gesture. Raising the
chalice, she steps into the circle
with conviction and truth in
her heart, and speaks the words
of summoning."*
*Lots of obscure and esoteric
imagery here. Harpocrates is
the Greek name for the Egyptian
god-child, Horus — the son
of Isis and Osiris. He is seen
as many things, including
the god of silence (a hermetic
interpretation) and also a direct
link to your holy guardian angel.*

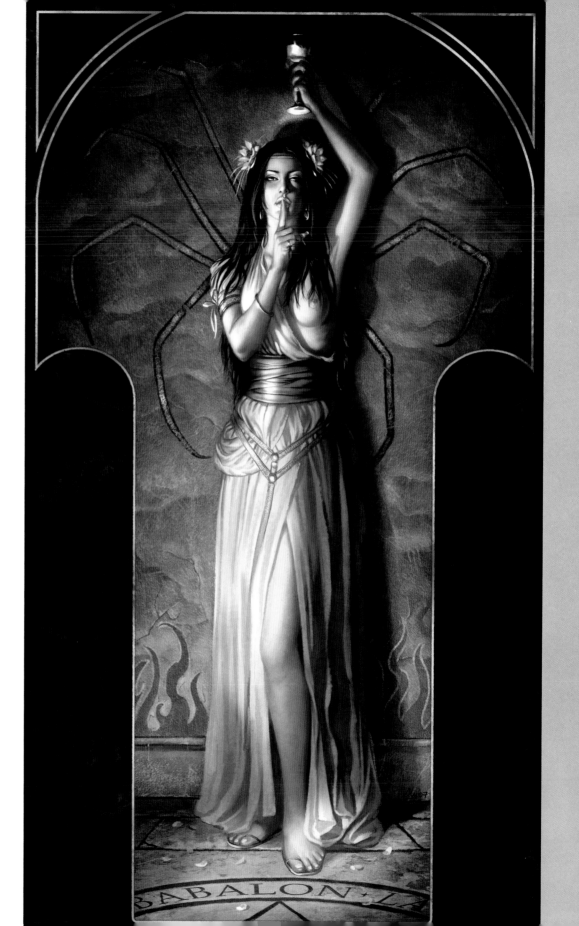

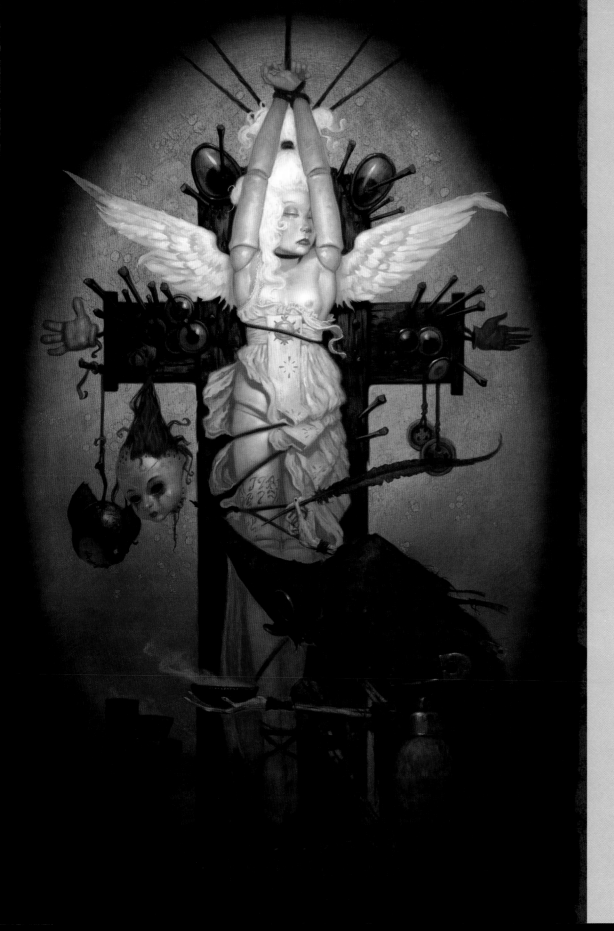

◀ **Angel**
Brom
Book illustration: *The Plucker*
from Abrams
Traditional media
www.bromart.com

The Plucker *is a novel, written
and illustrated by Brom. It's a
dark tale of a jack-in-the-box,
and his battle against an evil
force known as The Plucker.
Brom's strong use of design can
be seen in full force in this dark
and unnerving image from the
book, recalling the classics of
fairytale storytelling.*

▶ **Styx**
Cyril Van Der Haegen
Adobe Photoshop and
Corel Painter
www.tegehel.org

*The Styx is a river in Hades,
guarded by Phlegyas. Phlegyas'
boat of the damned is sailing
toward fresh souls deposed on a
monticule in the middle of the
river, while restless undeads are
hopelessly attracted by what
they used to be. The flags are
naval representations of their
respective countries, and indeed,
form a political comment.*

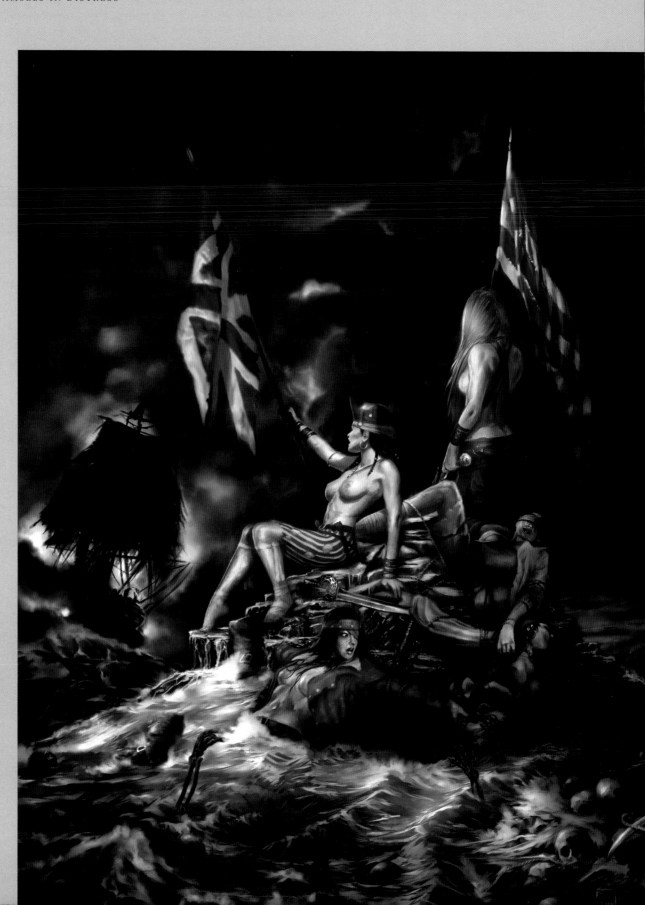

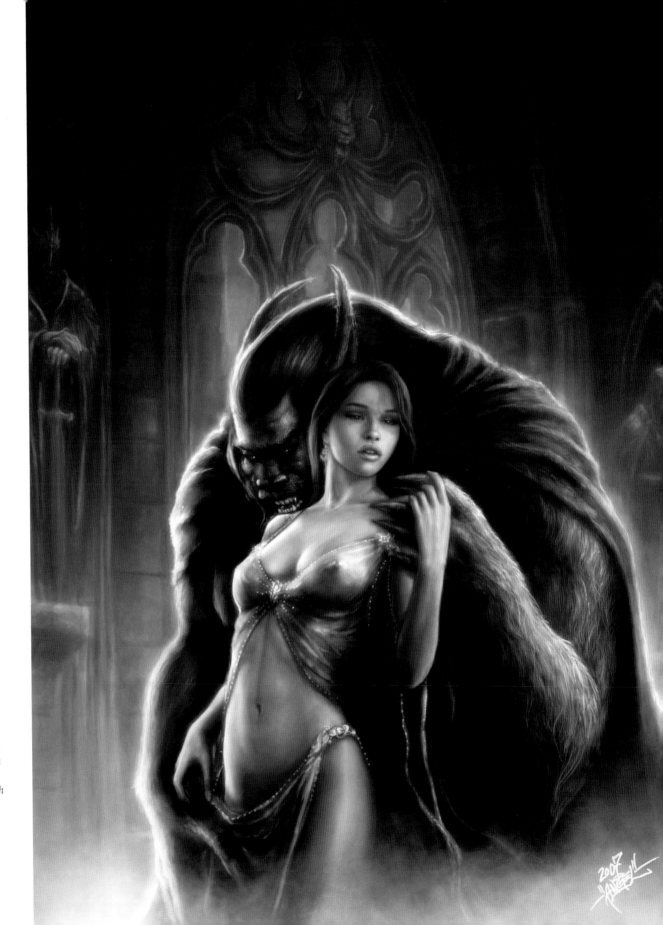

▶ Dark Romance
Sacha (Angel) Diener
Portfolio piece
Adobe Photoshop
www.angel3d.ch

*The moon broke through the
darkness, revealing a scene
painted in flesh, fur and silver.
She felt the brush of hot breath
on the back of her neck. Her
heart was pounding wildly with
desire and fear as she felt the
touch of his razor sharp claw
on her shoulder. The light was
cold as ice, the power of his
body so close to hers — both
melting into the night.*

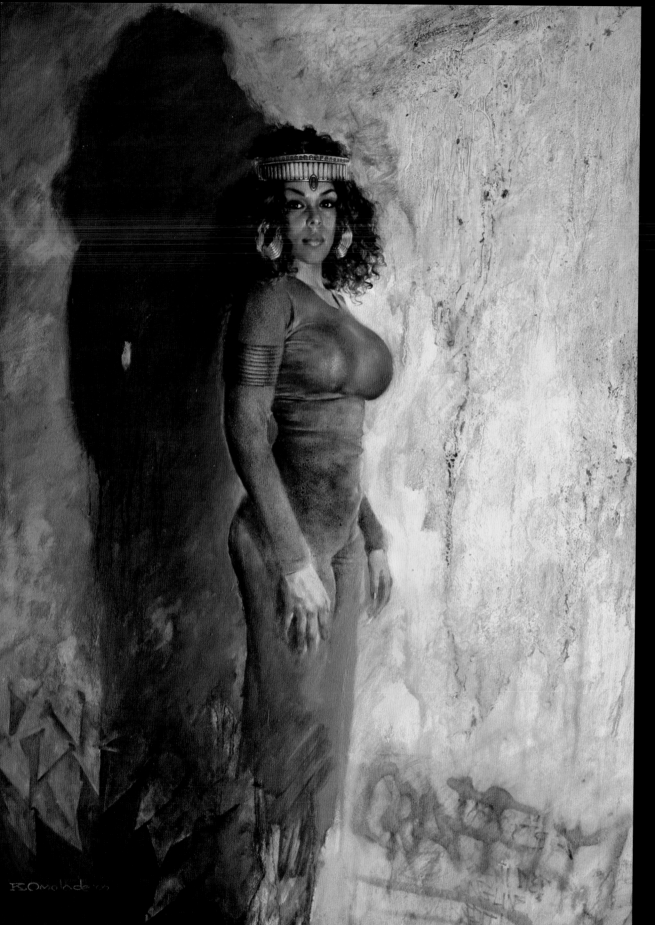

◀ **Metamorphosis**
Kip Omolade
Portfolio piece
Traditional media
www.kipomolade.com

Egyptian Graffiti III: Metamorphosis juxtaposes several painting styles. As a former graffiti artist I am fascinated with the way paint drips from spray paint or markers. This fascination has continued with my use of oil paint. Egyptian Graffiti III is part of a series of paintings that marry graffiti aesthetics (arrows, drips, lettering) with traditional representational painting The beauty of painting is that something forms from nothing. Brushstrokes of paint create the illusion of realism. The figure seems to form before the viewer's eyes, but "she" is not a beautiful buxom princess, she is paint.

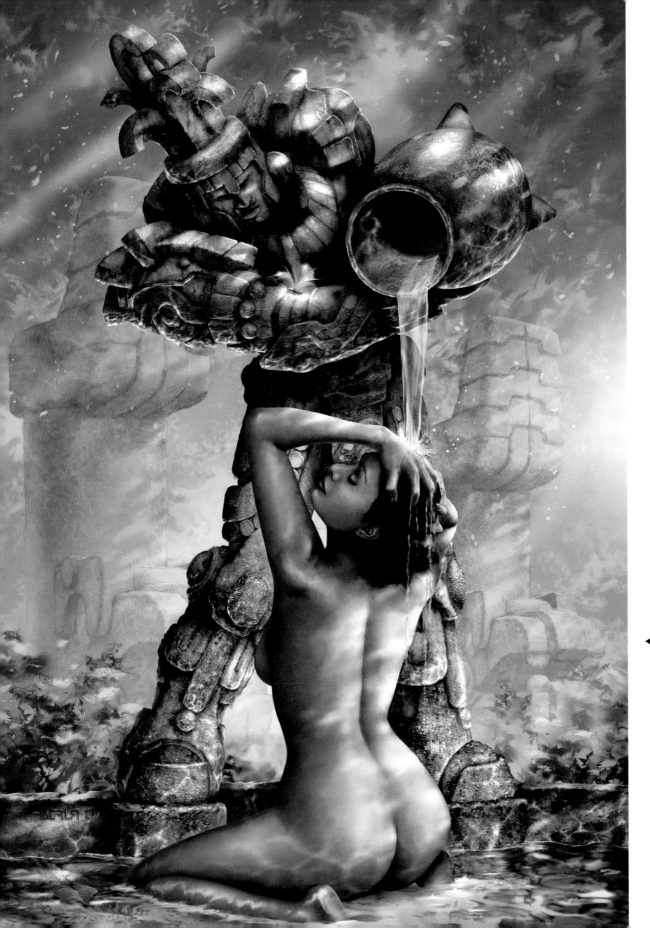

◄ **Agua de Jade**
Raul Cruz
Portfolio piece
Adobe Photoshop
www.racrufi.com

*Raul originally developed this
piece in his sketchbook and
describes his intentions for the
finished piece: "This work was
born in my sketch notebook
about two years ago. I wanted
to represent a fantasy scene in
the middle of dense vegetation,
where a beautiful woman bathes
in a water source, with a form
of futuristic soldier."*

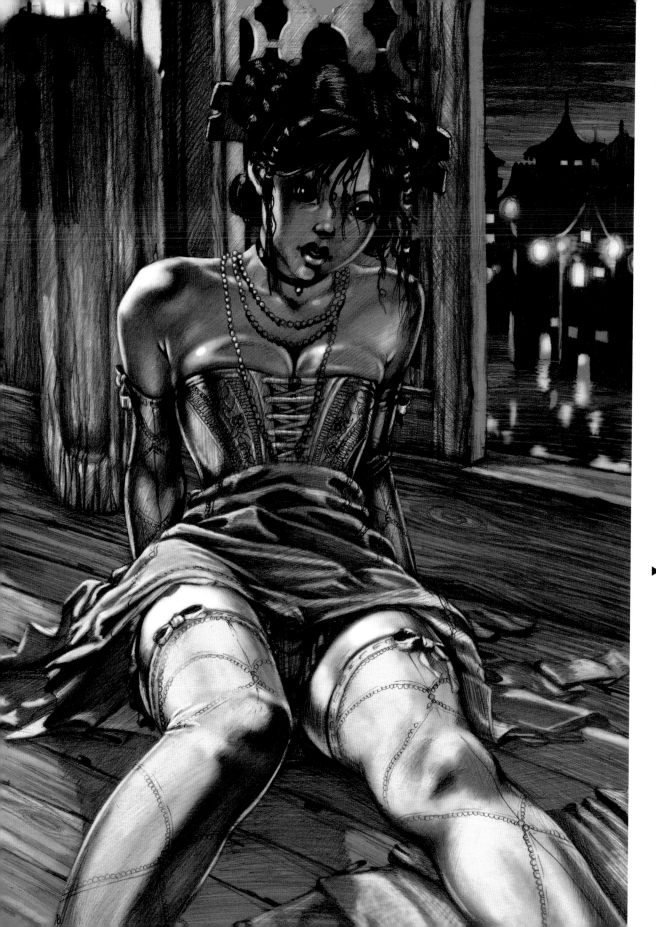

Canaltown Princess
Andy Hepworth
Portfolio piece
Corel Painter and pencil
www.andyhepworth.com

Andy produces intricately detailed pencil drawings that benefit from digital manipulation. "This was one of the first images I produced where I was experimenting with digital tone over a tight pencil drawing—a technique which has become my mainstay for monochrome illustration," he says. "I wanted to combine a kind of reality with some Asian pop-culture style."

Spangled 'n Tangled
Fastner & Larson
Mixed media, traditional and digital
www.fastnerandlarson.com

If hair bondage is the next frontier, we're ready! How convoluted can these things get? This painting started out as a pencil drawing by Rich (Larson) that was scanned, optimized in Photoshop, and then printed out on ordinary bond paper. Steve (Fastner) painted directly on this printout, using an assortment of grey magic markers, airbrush, gouache, and white colored pencil. He then scanned that image and added color digitally in Photoshop. It became the back cover of Rich Larson's "Bed & Bondage".

Midnight Tea
Fastner & Larson
Book illustration:
Little Black Book 3 from F&L
www.fastnerandlarson.com

*While (as yet) on the sidelines
in the whole cats-with-wings
phenomenon, we find a well-
placed fairy or two can lend a
wholly undeserved cachet to our
otherwise frothy frittatas. Add
a cup of the world's only really
civilized beverage, and we're
ready for induction into the
Royal Academy—assuming
our bribe finds its way into
the right hands!*

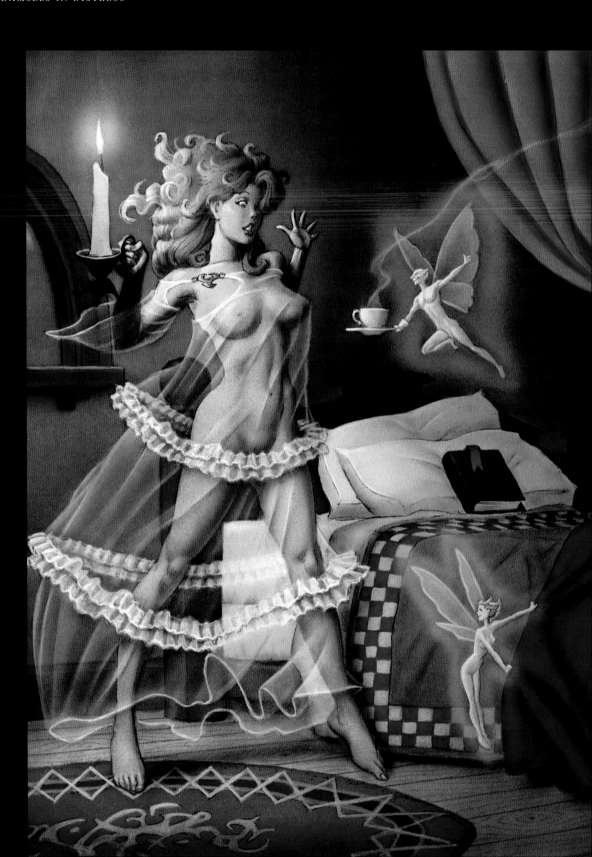

◀ **The Albatrose**
Arthur Suydam
Promotional poster
Oil over ink
www.arthursuydam.com

This piece — completed as a promotional poster — is a wonderfully entertaining painting from Arthur. The proud pirate queen bears a passing resemblance to a certain film star, while the circling seagulls could be looking for pickings off the rather glutinous crew!

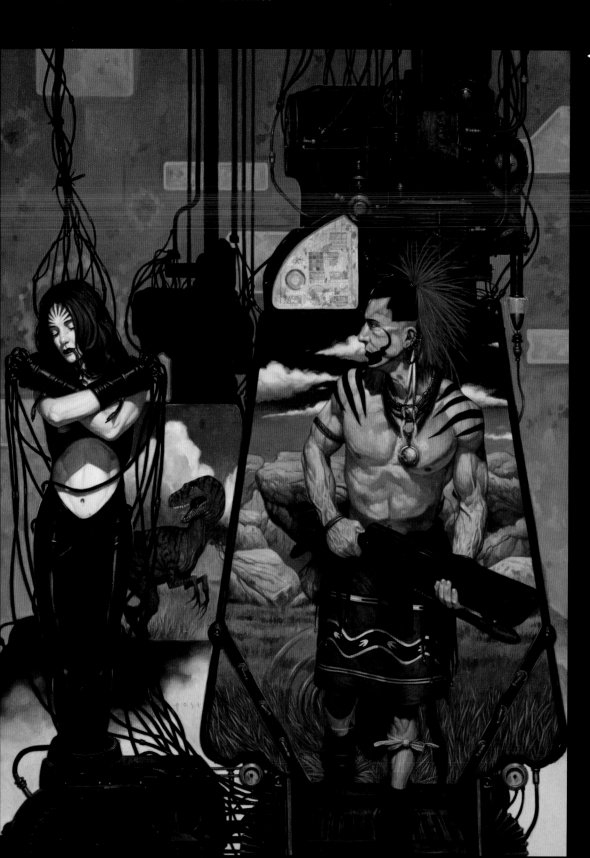

◀ **Tangents**
R.K. Post
Book cover: *Wizards of the Coast*
Digital media
www.rkpost.net

*A book cover showing infinite
possibilities while traveling in
time and space. The units are
powered by the bondage maven,
peacefully giving her essence to
science and bloodshed.*

Dragon Girl
Mark Harrison
Abaddon Books/Rebellion
Digital media
www.2000ad.org/markus/

The (literally) bloody Dragon girl gave me cause for concern. She's just escaped from the Dragon Worm's maw by freeing herself from her father's oversized armor (well, that's my story). She's not getting out of that mouth without a few scratches. The image itself owes a little to an Ingrid Bergman film poster for **Joan of Arc** and a favorite painting by Frank Frazetta — **At the Earth's Core** — of a slave girl in a milky pool threatened by Mahars. Artistically, the water acts as a natural cropping device, and its other properties aren't lost on the female form either... As a foundation I used a photo-composite and a CG model worm built in Zbrush.

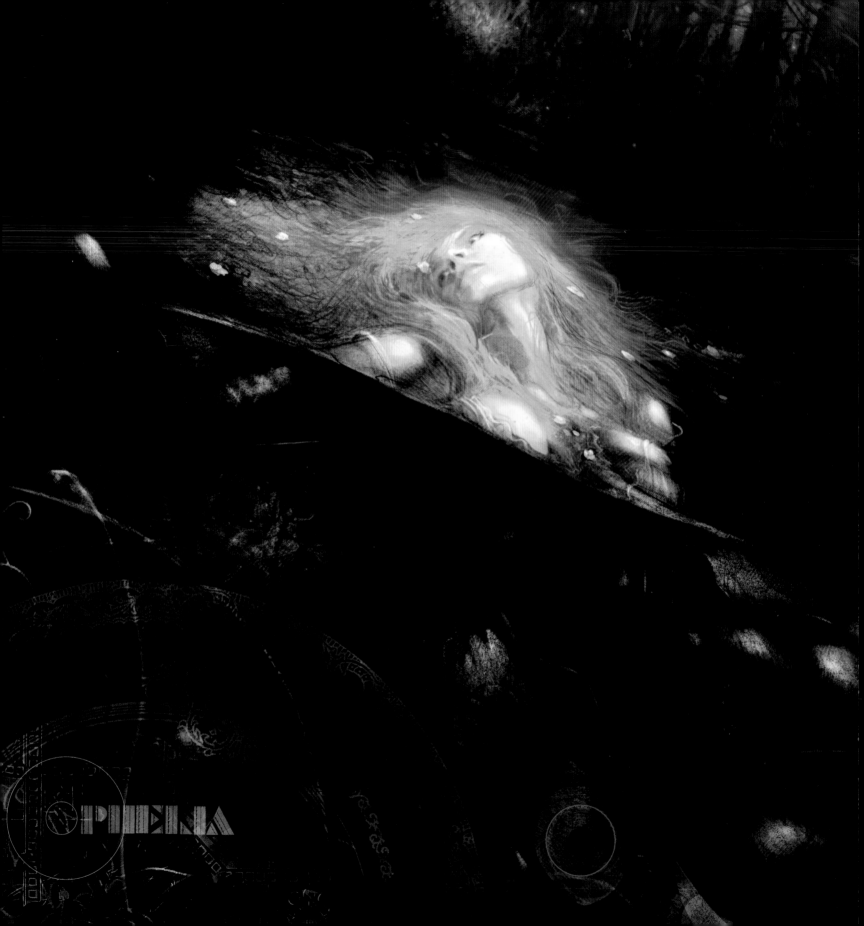

OPHELIA

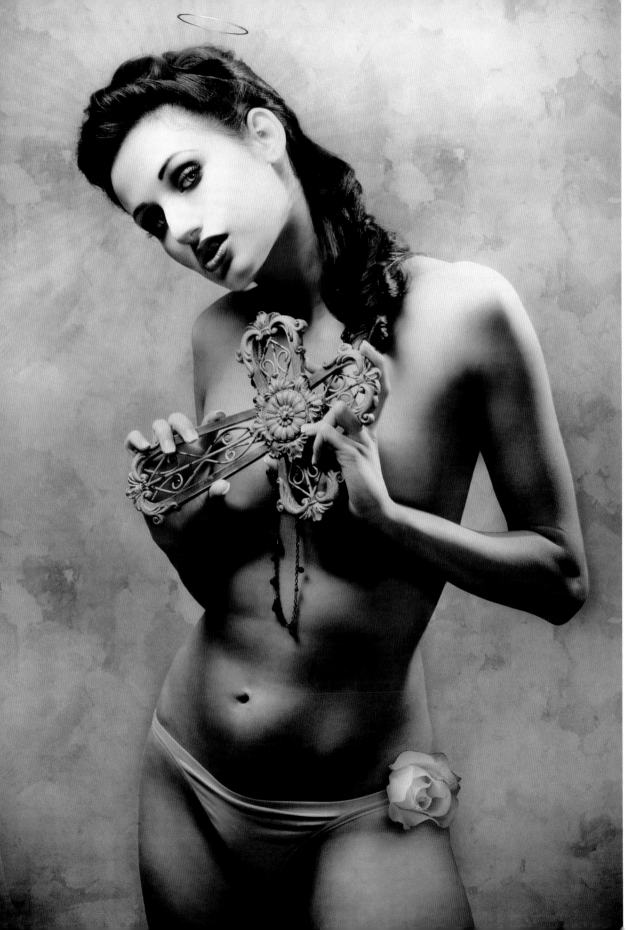

◀◀ **Ophelia**
Glen Angus
www.gangus.net

Born of a crude and loose sketch, I always wanted to create my own interpretation of this very popular and famous subject matter: Ophelia drowning from sorrow at the loss of love from Shakespeare's Hamlet. I wanted this piece to have an eerie, but still somewhat sensual feel to it.

◀ **Saint Amie**
Chad Michael Ward
Portfolio piece
Adobe Photoshop

Chad creates darkly erotic artwork from his studio photographs, with additional digital manipulation in Adobe Photoshop. His scantily clad "Saint Amie" is bestowed with a crucifix, rosary beads and halo, while exuding a less-than-saintly sex appeal. "This piece was created for my upcoming book, tentatively titled "Dangerous Beauties." I wanted to do several religious-themed images featuring beautiful women.

CHAPTER 3

WANTON WITCHES AND SEXY SORCERESSES

◀ **Siri—The Princess**
Bjorn Hurri
Portfolio piece
Adobe Photoshop
www.bjornhurri.com

Bjorn created paintings
specifically for this book.
"When I was asked if I wanted
to participate in this book I
knew right away that I wanted
to contribute this piece. I see her
as a princess of a harem sheikh,
sensual and capable of putting
her guests under spells. Her pet
is a 'water win', a mythical
dragon that flies just above
the water's surface."

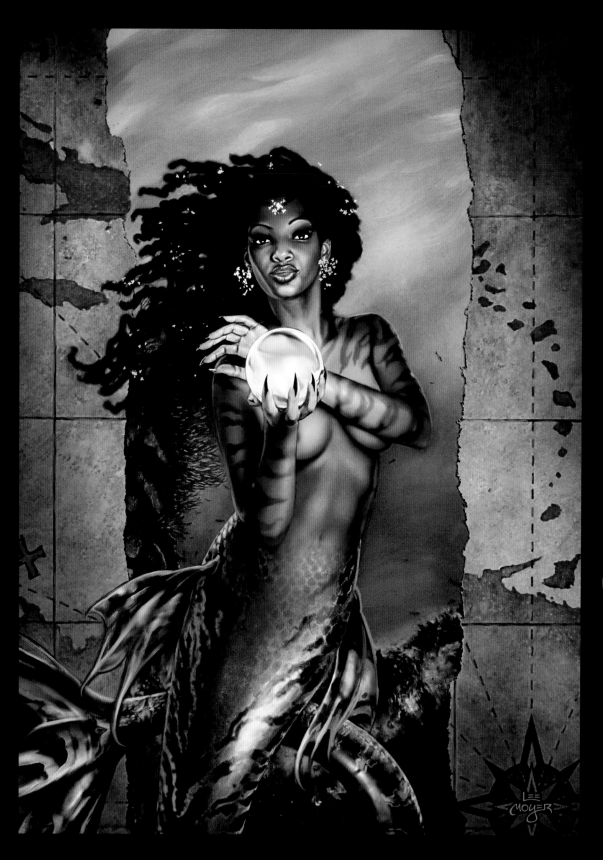

◀ **Port Royale**
Lee Moyer
Portfolio piece
Pencil, acrylic, Adobe Photoshop
www.leemoyer.com

As a lover of fantasy and science fiction, I'm struck by how pale and uninteresting the protagonists tend to be portrayed — particularly given the diverse readership these genres enjoy. I had originally intended to show a jet-black mermaid off the Skeleton Coast of Namibia, but luckily found a wonderful Jamaican model named Royale instead. Port Royale was considered the richest and wickedest city in the world before it sank into the sea. Royale's name and personality gave the piece a more romantic and piratical direction.

▶ **Conjure Maitz**
Don Maitz
Book cover: *First Maitz*
Ursus Publishing
Oil
www.paravia.com/DonMaitz

A lonely sorcerer has discovered a recipe that summons beautiful companions. He gives a new meaning to "making a date!" Creating paintings can be a magical experience, and the title I chose carries a dual interpretation. I signed the painting in the book of magic on the page that provides the conjury.

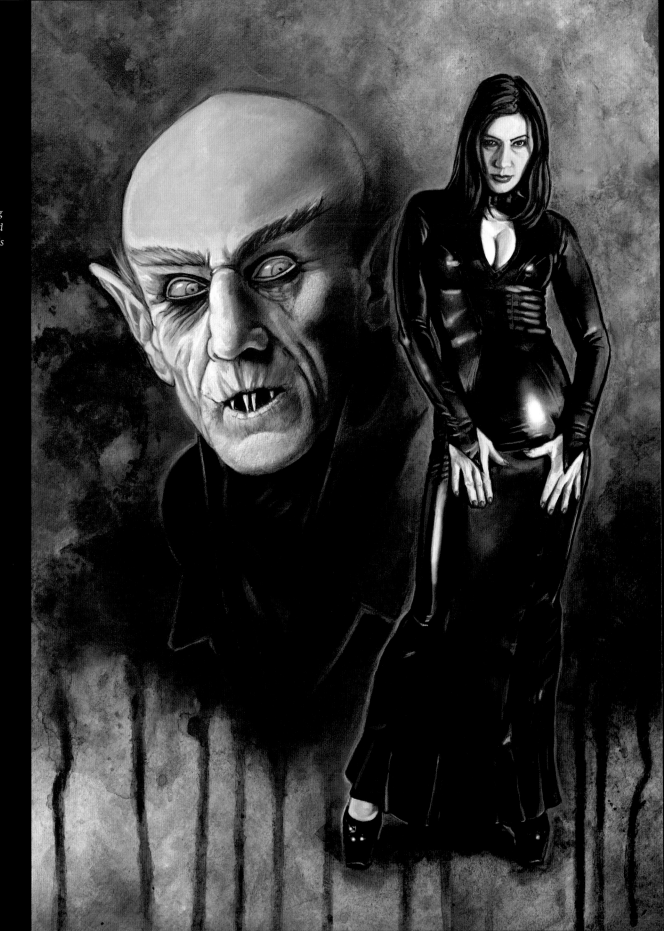

▶ **Ivy Blue and Nosferatu**
Ric Frane
Personal piece
Acrylic
www.ricfrane.com

*This is one of the first of my
"Monster with a pin-up"
paintings. I was planning on
just doing a vampire painting
of the model, Ivy Blue, but had
the idea to team up my models
with classic movie monsters.
Who could match Ivy in her
shiny rubber dress...?*

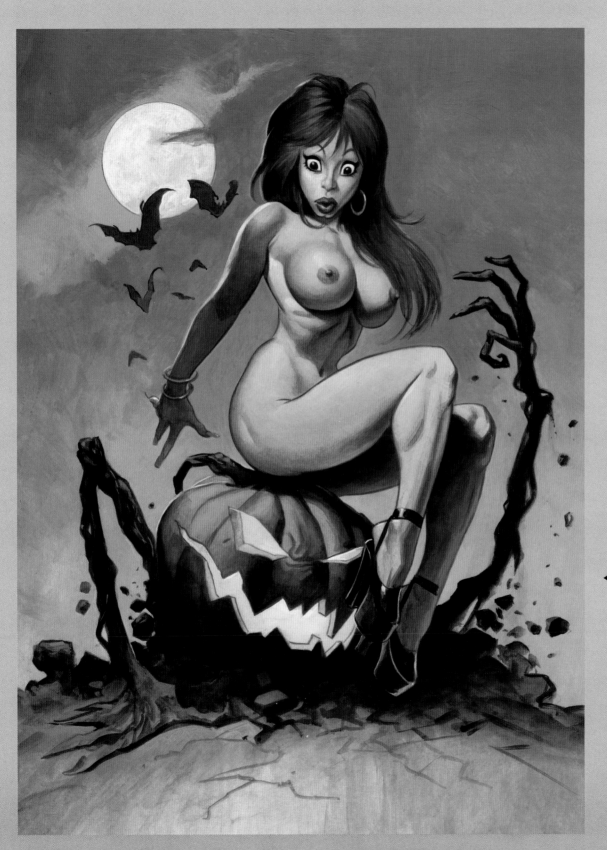

◄ **Stacy & Her Pumpkin**
Alex Horley
Portfolio Piece
Acrylic
www.alexhorley.com

This was done for our annual Halloween greeting card. For some reason, it took a more "cartoony" direction than my usual works. At times I like to play with styles, like mixing Disney-like features with more "realistic" painted renderings. It was an experiment that many people responded well to. They really seem to love the humor in it.

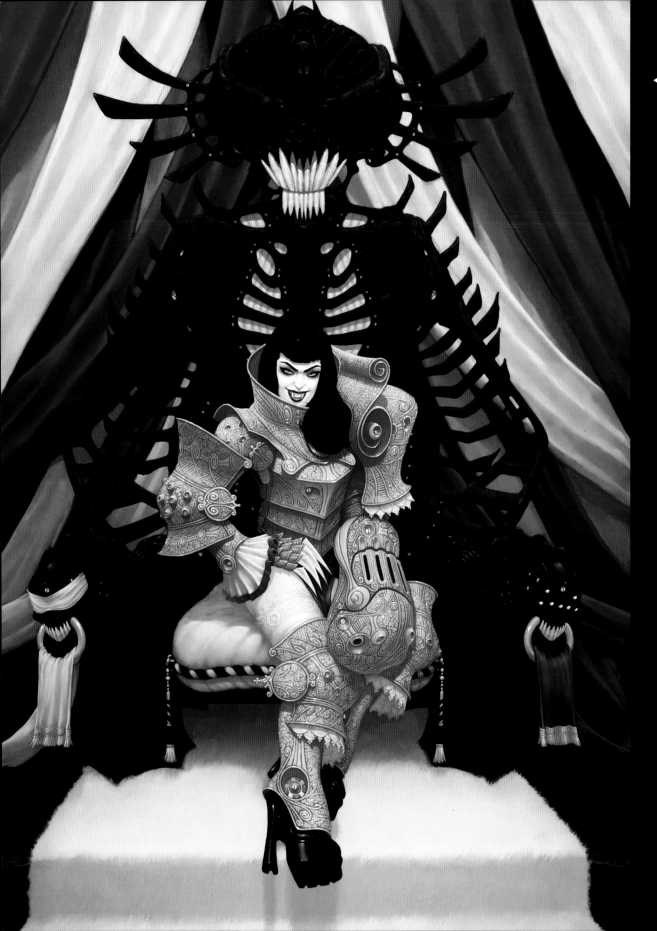

◄ **Soul Drinker**
Malachai Maloney (Liquidwerx)
Personal piece
Digital media
www.liquidwerx.com

*This is one of the many Blackjack
Betty incarnations that have
come to life over the last three
years. This Blackjack Betty
variant dwells in an alternate
reality, where technology is
fueled by magic. She exists as
an ancient vampire queen,
who feeds on the souls of the
human inhabitants of her
world. Opulence and evil are
the underlying themes.*

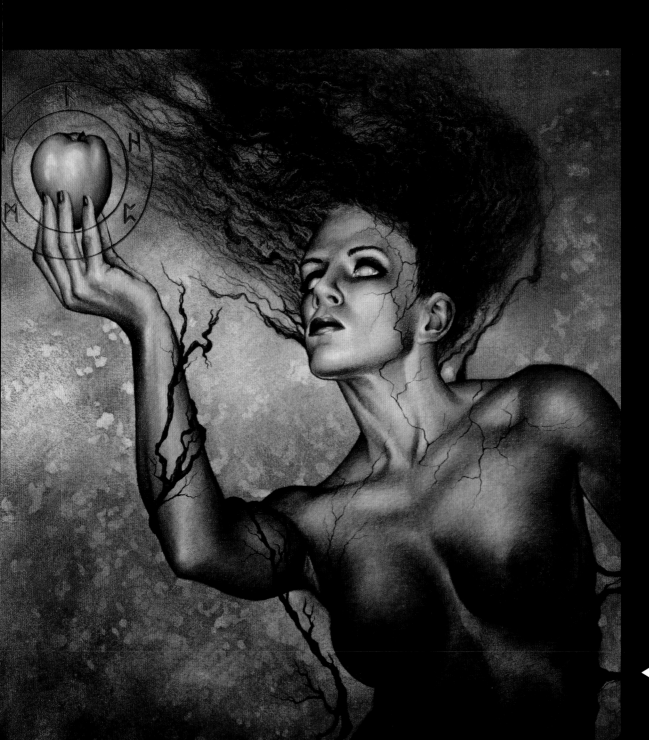

◄ **Becoming**
Matt Hughes
Portfolio piece
Colored pencil, watercolor on
watercolor paper

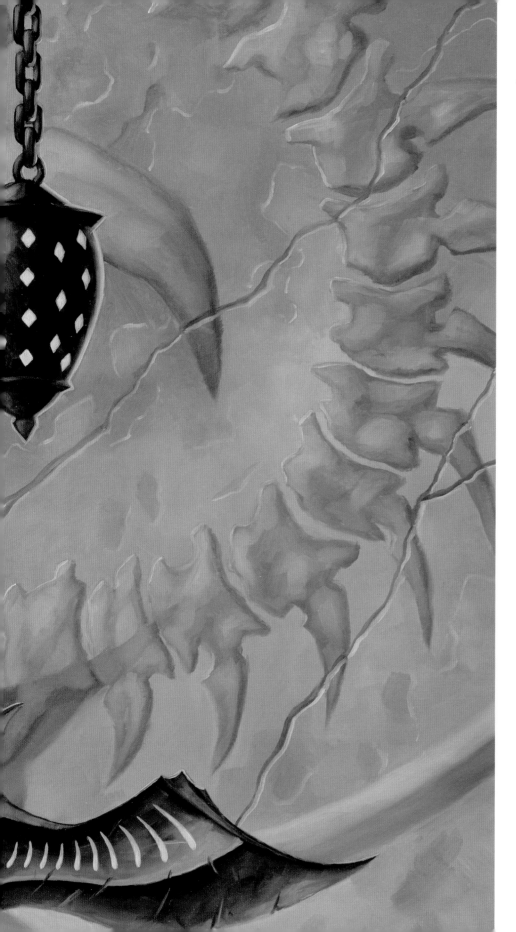

◀ **Wraith Queen**
Matt Wilson
Illustration for
WARMACHINE: Apotheosis
Privateer Press
Character Trademark Privateer
Press, Inc. 2005
Oil on board
www.mattwilsonart.com

Nowadays, I'm like the Judge Dredd of painters. Instead of "Judge, Jury, and Executioner", I'm "Artist, Art Director, and Publisher" of my own work. The Wraith Queen is a character I created for the miniatures game, Warmachine, which has been my personal playground for the last five years. After working for so long on other peoples' projects, it's very liberating to be in total control of the creative process, and to know that no one is going to pull the rug out from under you at the last second!

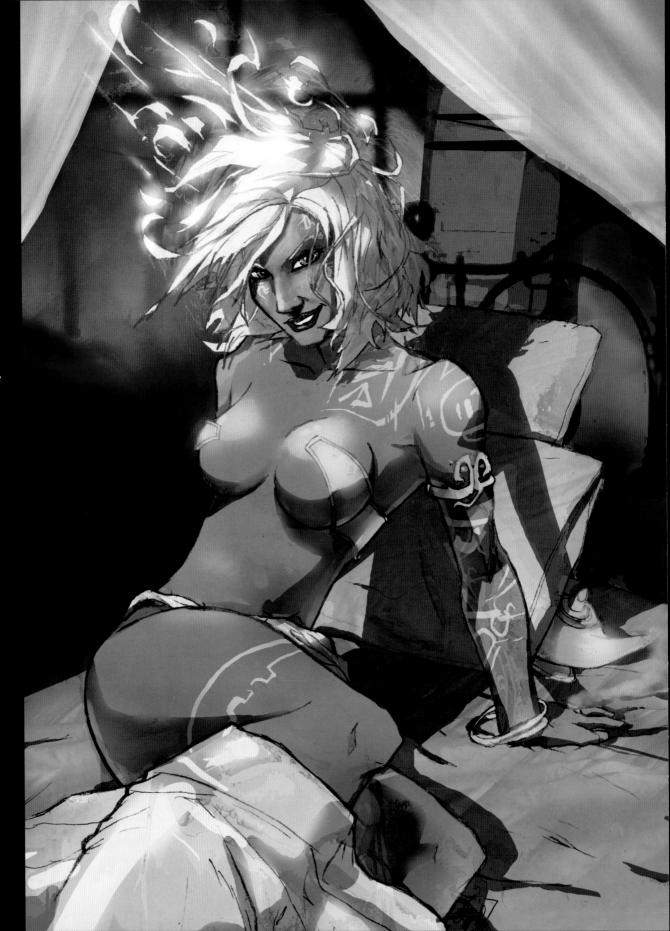

Djinn
David Cousens
Publication piece
Pencils and Adobe Photoshop
www.CoolSurface.com

The mythology of the djinn has been a popular theme in art and literature for centuries. In this modern take on the subject matter, David presents a female djinn to entice the viewer. As he explains, "The race of the 'Djinn' were born from a smokeless fire, invisible to humans until they chose to make their presence known. Female djinn were renowned for their alluring nature and ability to seduce any person they chose…"

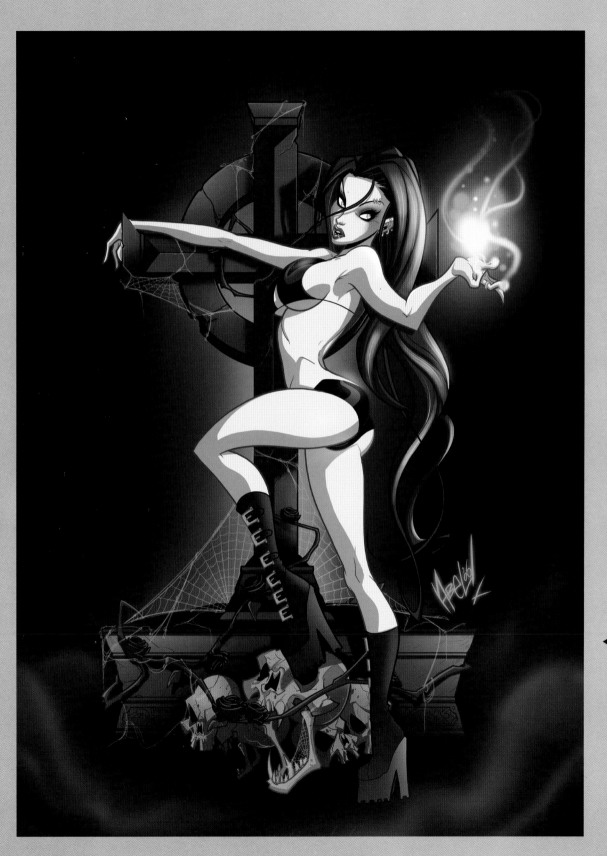

◀ **Twenty Four**
Martin Abel
Picture Premium magazine
Digital Media: Adobe Photoshop,
Alias Sketchbook Pro
www.martinabel.com

*In this image the girl has
a strong dynamic pose that
recalls classic pin-up art.
Is this her grave, or merely
a passing stop-over? Martin's
quirky gothic imagery is
shown to full effect here.*

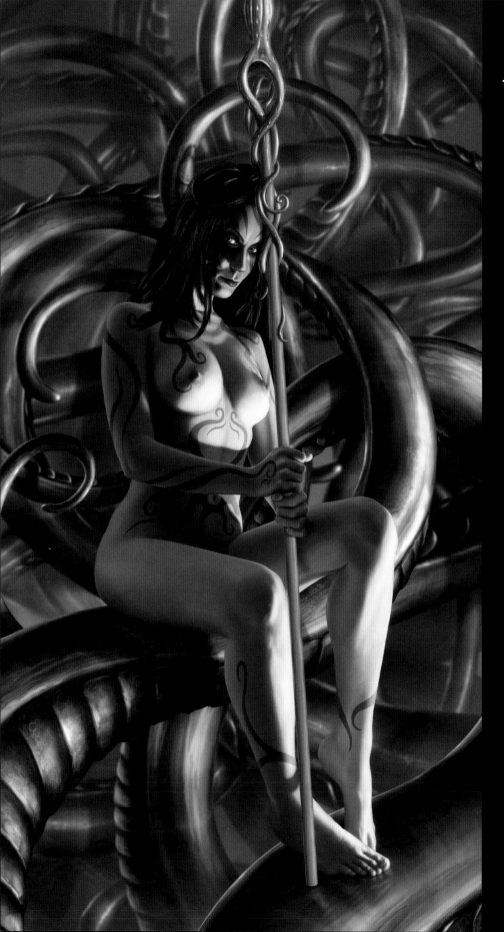

◀ **Goh Cephal**
Henning Ludvigsen
Portfolio piece
Adobe Photoshop
www.henningludvigsen.com

*Dark art has always inspired
me, and I wanted to create
something within the lines of the
Cthulhu mythos setting—only
taking a few major steps further
in the direction of eroticism. It's
easy to tip over with a painting
like this and end up making it
somewhat tasteless. I tried to
make her appear strong and in
control of the massive tentacle
beast, and feel I succeeded.*

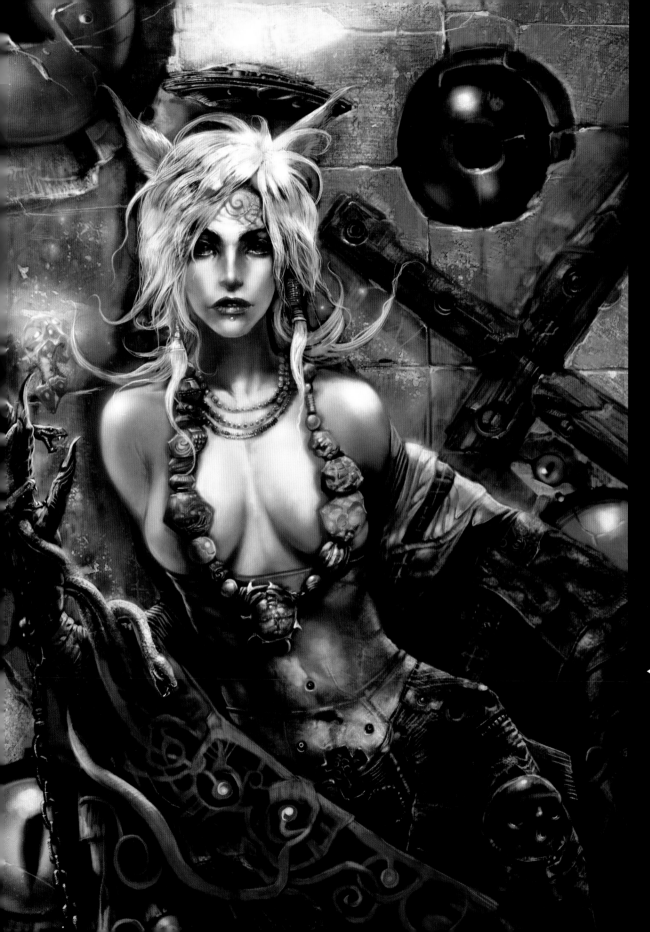

◀ **Witchery**
Kuang Hong
Portfolio piece
Adobe Photoshop
www.zemotion.net

*An intricately detailed piece
from Kuang Hong. The central
character is surrounded by
the tools of her trade and
other elements that imply the
title of the work. Organic and
technological themes combine
to great effect, all rendered
with a real professionalism.*

▶ **The 3 Muses**
Andrew Jones
Live painting for LA fashion show
Client: Skin Graft Designs
Digital (Corel Painter X)
www.androidjones.com

*Andrew Jones is gaining a
reputation for his experimental
and innovative approach, and
for taking fantasy art to new
audiences. "This was another live
painting I created for the Skin
Graft boys in Los Angeles. It was
playing while the models ran
down the runway. As payment
for the gig they are designing
me a custom leather-and-fur
Wacom guitar strap!"*

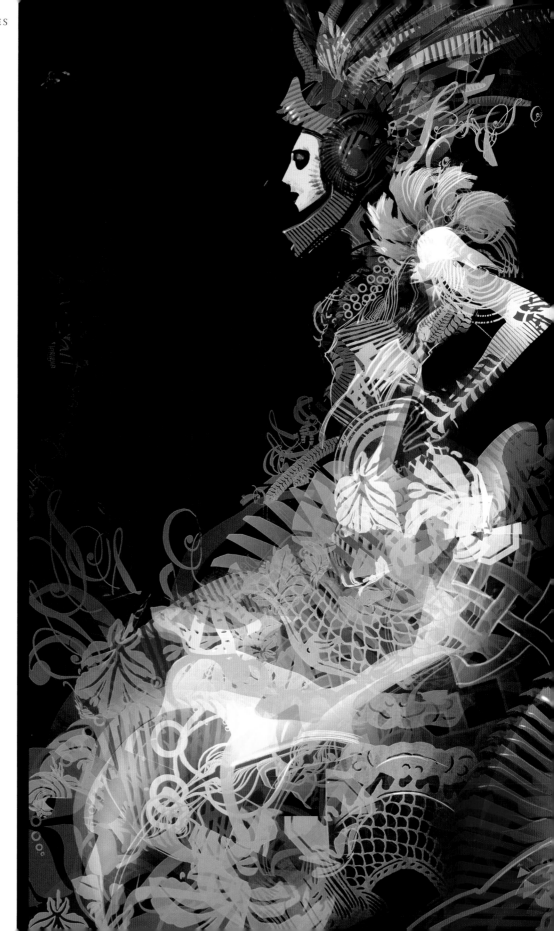

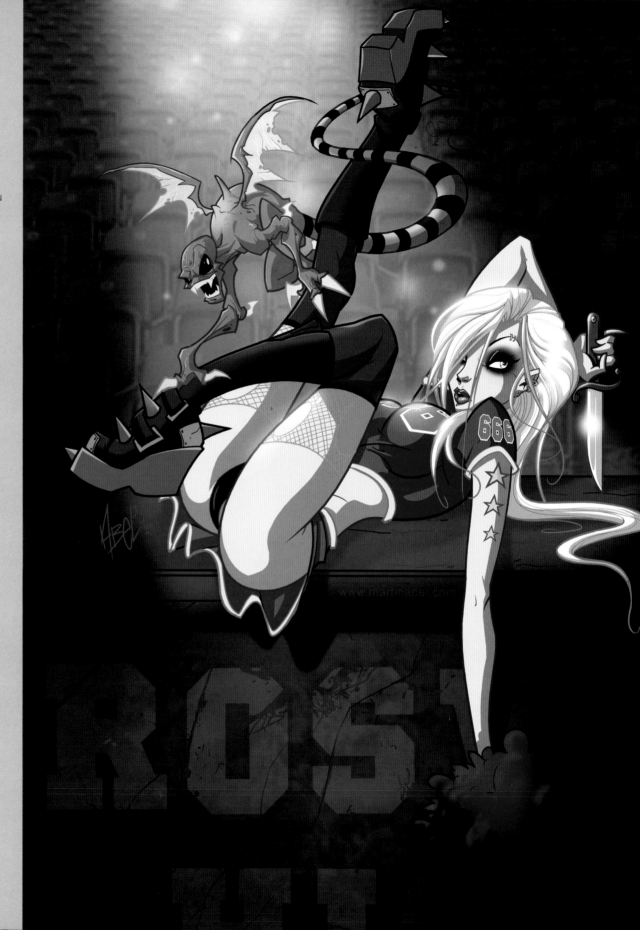

▶ **Roswell High**
Martin Abel
Illustration: *Picture Premium*
Digital media: Adobe Photoshop,
Alias Sketchbook Pro and
www.martinabel.com

Martin completed this as a full-page magazine pin-up and it's a good example of his gothic girls; all innocent and knowing at the same time. This lass attends Roswell High School, and her sexy cheerleader uniform adds to the playfulness of this image.

▶ Red Ribbons
Tony Mauro
Portfolio piece
Adobe Photoshop
www.darkdayproductions.com

This piece has actually sparked a new series for me — I like the style and want to do a 4 to 6 image series based on this look. My goal was to do something a little more "design-y", for lack of a better word. It breaks the mould a little bit from what I ordinarily do with my environments and backgrounds, so I had fun with this one. The model is a good friend of mine, Jennifer, who always comes through for me in a pinch when I need a good model.

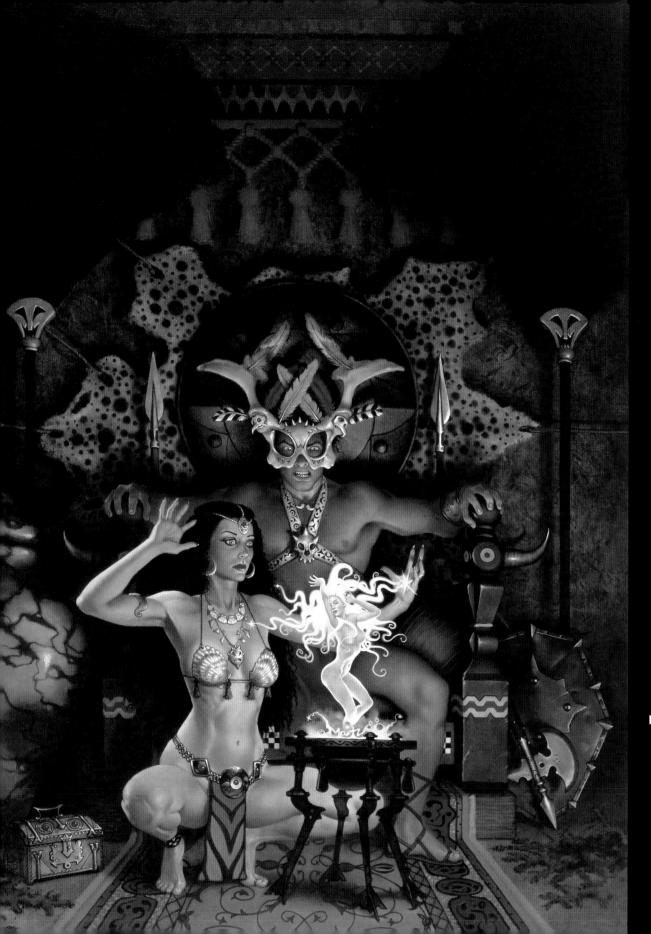

The Oracle
Don Maitz
Book cover: *The Oracle*
Popular Library
Oil
www.paravia.com/DonMaitz

A sorceress is commanded to entertain a barbarian warlord. The barbarian's headdress and chest-piece costume were created from cow's bone by the model.

▶ **Dreamcatcher Prostasia**
Johann de Venecia
Portfolio piece
Adobe Photoshop

I wanted to create a high-class prostitute in a twisted reality, where the filthy rich pay not just for "basic" services, but more importantly for what comes after: a guilt-free slumber, devoid of bad dreams.

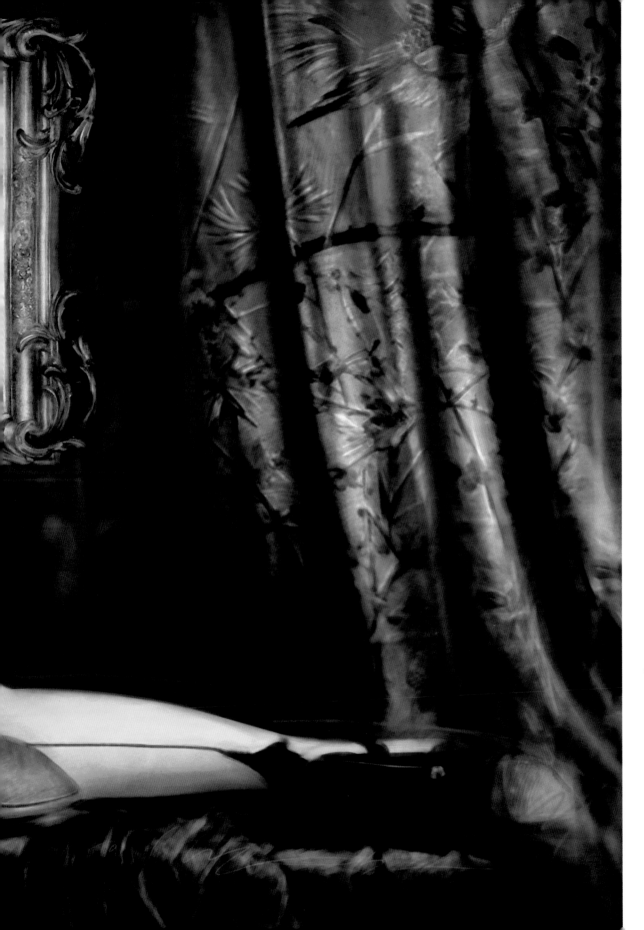

◀ **Recline**
Alan Daniels
Portfolio piece
Acrylic, chalk and oil on
canvas board
www.heavenlyhusseys.com

*The girl in this image seems aloof
and detached, seeing herself as
more of a work of art than the
painting she lies opposite. Alan
uses mixed media to great effect
and the detailing in this image
is quite striking — particularly
on the cloth.*

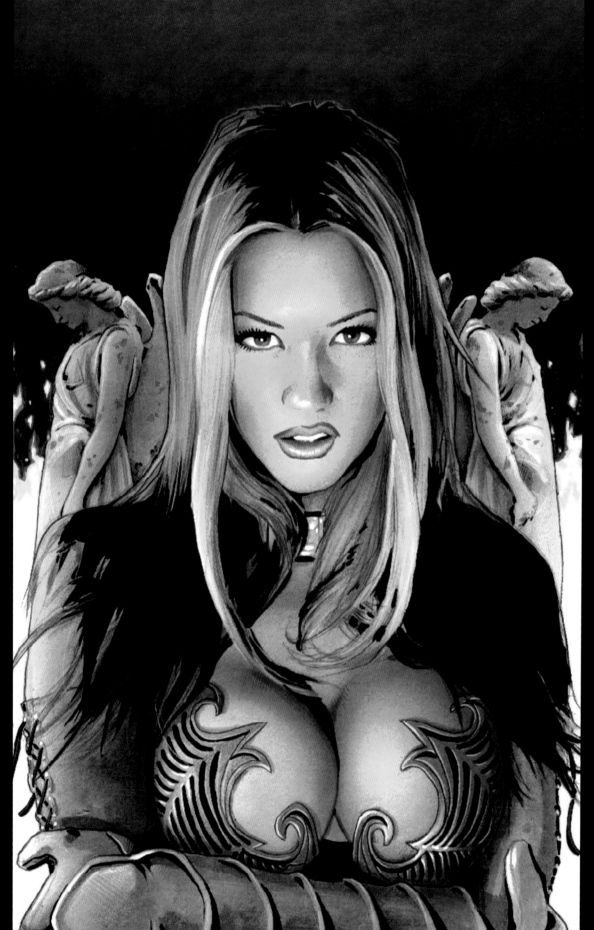

◀ **Statuesque**
Matt Busch
Portfolio piece
Acrylic and prismacolor
www.mattbusch.com

The lovely Alley Baggett is the model for this stunning piece, rendered by notorious illustrator Matt Busch. Alley and Matt met, of all places, at a comic book convention in Ohio, and soon began collaborating on dozens of pieces, including work for a comic book called "Alleycat". The simplicity of the symmetrical design is what draws you in, but it's the subtle nuances and details that keep your eyes glued to it. Busch used this image on the back of his business card, and it's no surprise that the piece has become a fan-favorite!

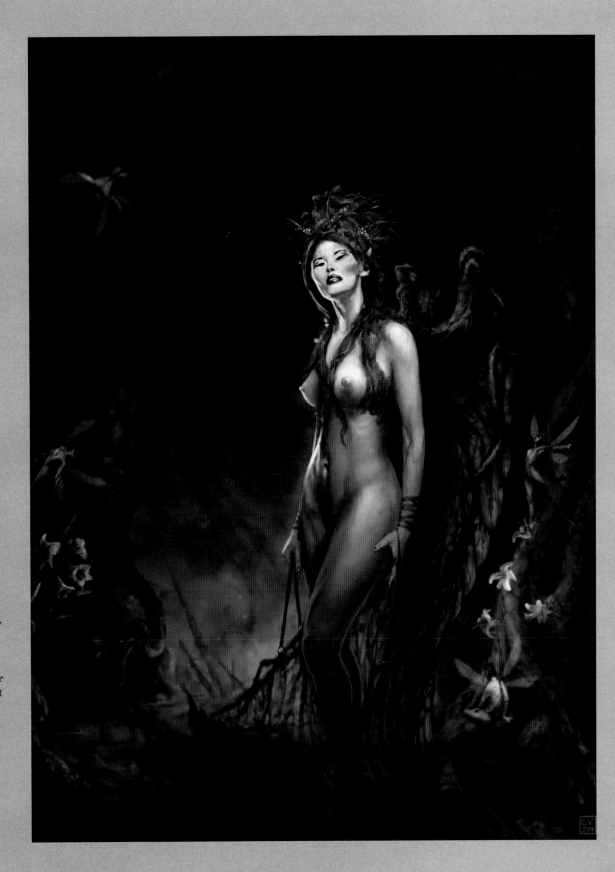

▶ **Sylvan Spirit**
Cyril Van Der Haegen
Portfolio piece
Digital media: Adobe Photoshop,
Corel Painter
www.tegehel.org

*Here, I simply wanted to create
a non-stereotypical wood spirit
with wings made of natural
elements found in a forest or
swamp area. While human in
appearance, I made her eyes
alien enough to have a feeling
of otherworldliness. She's also
looking down at the viewer
semi-defiantly, perhaps a
reminder of what humans
are doing to her habitat.*

▶ **Charge!**
Aly Fell
Competition Entry
Adobe Photoshop
www.darkrising.co.uk

"*Mary had to take dramatic steps to keep her hair up. Frankie loved it that way, but without Griffin Invisible Hold Hairspray she was stuck. Of course 40,000 volts helped a bit!*" Completed for a Thunderdome challenge on Concept Art.org

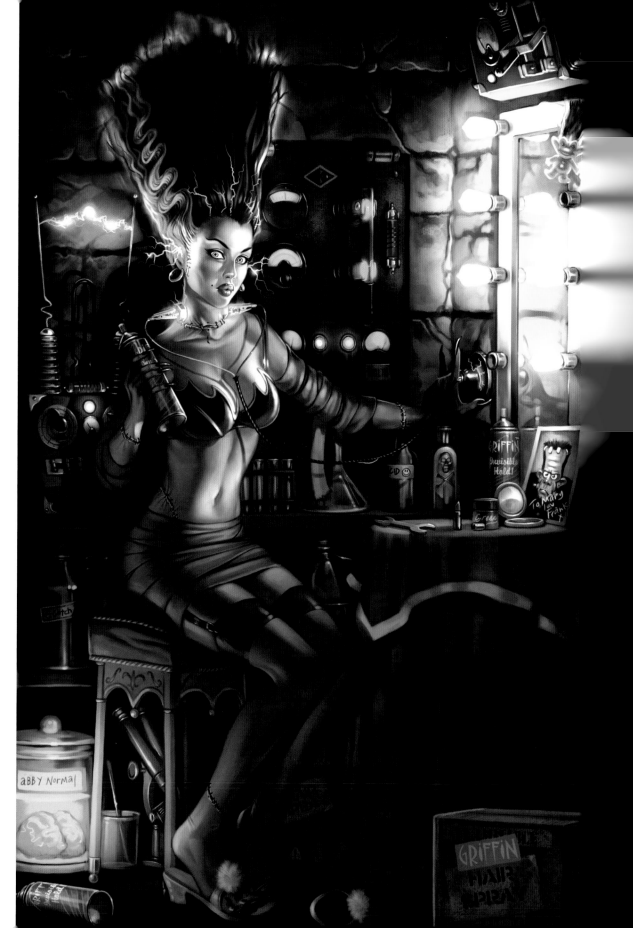

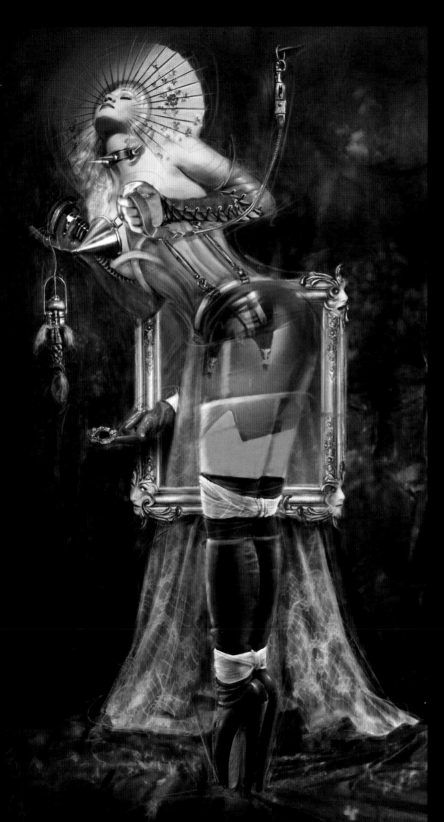

◀ **Curator**
Alan Daniels
Portfolio piece
Acrylic, chalk and oils on board
www.heavenlyhusseys.com

In this image, Alan presents us with a girl who collects other peoples' detritus, amalgamating the objects she finds into her own world, like a sort of human garbage collector.

▶   **Sensual Summoning**
Matt Busch
Portfolio piece
Acrylic and Prismacolor
www.mattbusch.com

Another knockout piece featuring the alluring Alley Baggett. This time, Matt Busch set the tone at the midnight hour, in a mystical graveyard. Busch is fond of using stark contrast in his imagery, not only in values, but in the content and subject matter itself. Here, Busch uses a sensual, smoldering beauty, and places her in a dark and mysterious setting. Yet Alley appears to be comfortable in her environment, and is no stranger to the darkness. Certainly she would be a welcome find, should you ever trespass into such a forbidden locale!

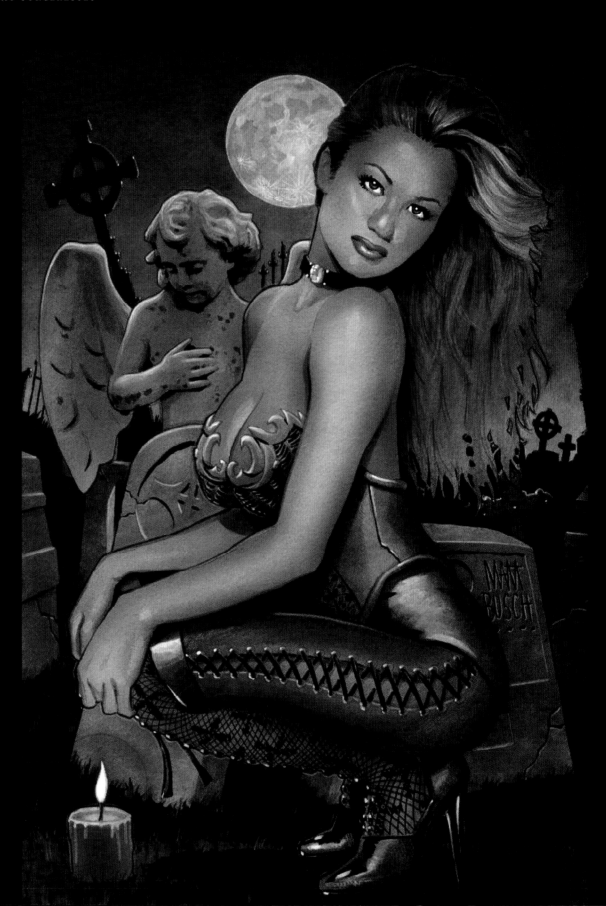

▶ **The Empress**
Bjorn Hurri
Self-promotion
Photoshop
www.bjornhurri.com

I see this woman as some sort of beast master; she has so much power that all living creatures are under her control. This painting was one of the more difficult to paint because I had problems deciding which way she should be facing. The final result was satisfying for me because the painting ended up being very interesting and gracious, yet powerful because I used my beautiful girlfriend as the model while painting it.

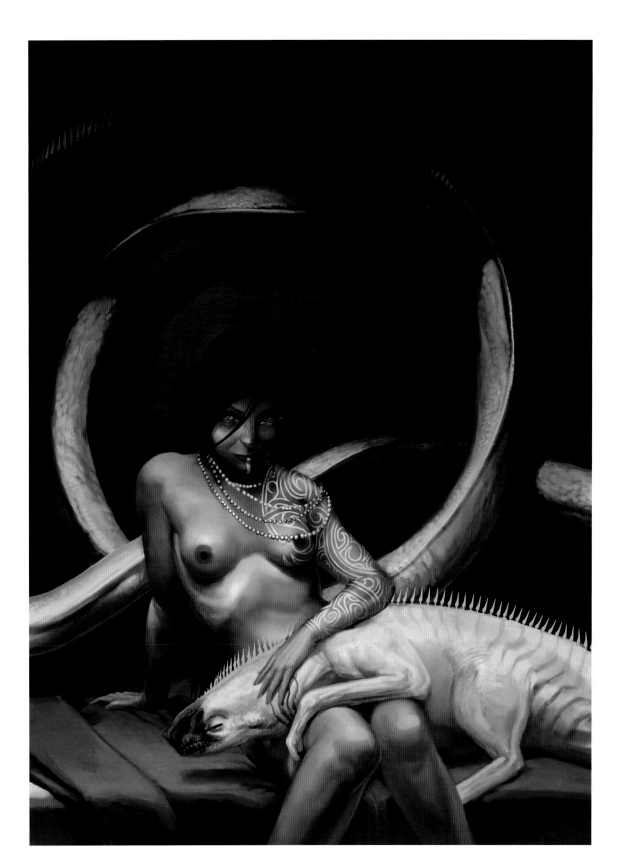

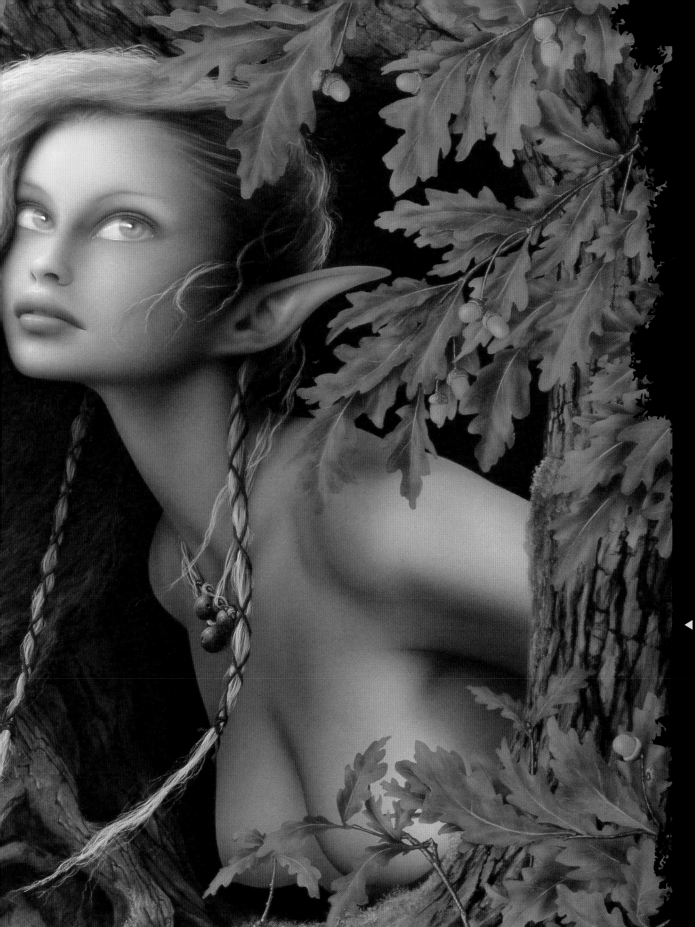

CHAPTER 4

FEMME FAIRIES AND EROTIC ELVES

The Dryad of the Oaks
Jim Burns
Portfolio piece
Acrylic and ink
www.jimburns.co.uk

This was a purely personal piece based loosely on a color sketch I created for my collection "IMAGO". The worlds of ancient mythology have always fascinated me—they occupied the same territory of the imagination as fairy tales and, latterly, science fiction and fantasy. The Dryad of the Oaks—an ancient Greek nymph of the woodlands—was a recent venture into this territory

▶ **The Harpy**
Daren Bader
Portfolio piece
www.darenbader.com

The Harpy started out as a series of scribbles and gestures with the intention of finding some sort of composition. When I ended up with a few sweeping lines that all seemed to point to the same spot, I thought "great place for a focal point!" From that moment on, it was just a bunch of scribbling and refining over and over until I thought I should stop. I like what da Vinci said; "Art is never finished, just abandoned".

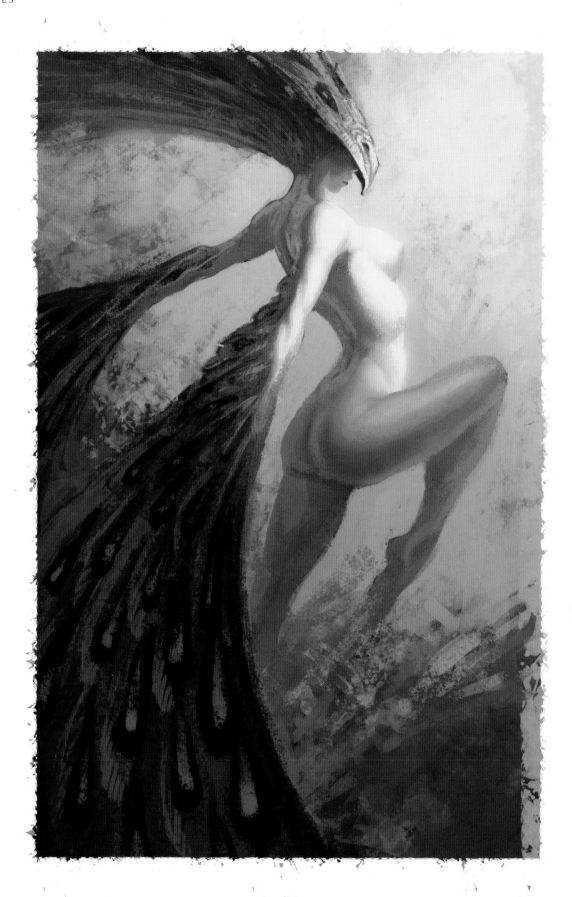

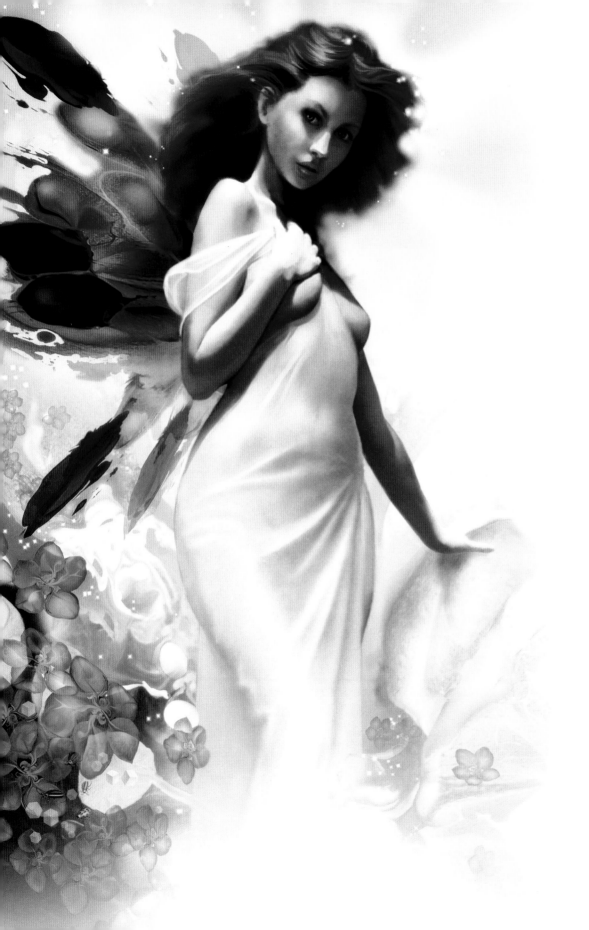

◄ **Lucy**
John Blumen
Portfolio piece
Digital media
www.portfolios.com/johnblumen

"Lucy" was created for inclusion in an illustration exhibition entitled "The Beatles Generation". I choose the song "Lucy in the Sky with Diamonds" for my entry. I tried to evoke the look of the period with the use of color and the psychedelic influences rather than the visual style of the time.

◄ **Zpheru's Gate**
Matt Hughes
Portfolio piece
Colored pencil and watercolor on
watercolor paper
www.MattHughesArt.com

*I have always been intrigued
by Asian art and felt this was a
perfect opportunity to produce a
three-dimensional Asian dragon.
Symbolism is abundant in this
image, but I will let the viewer
decide its final meaning!*

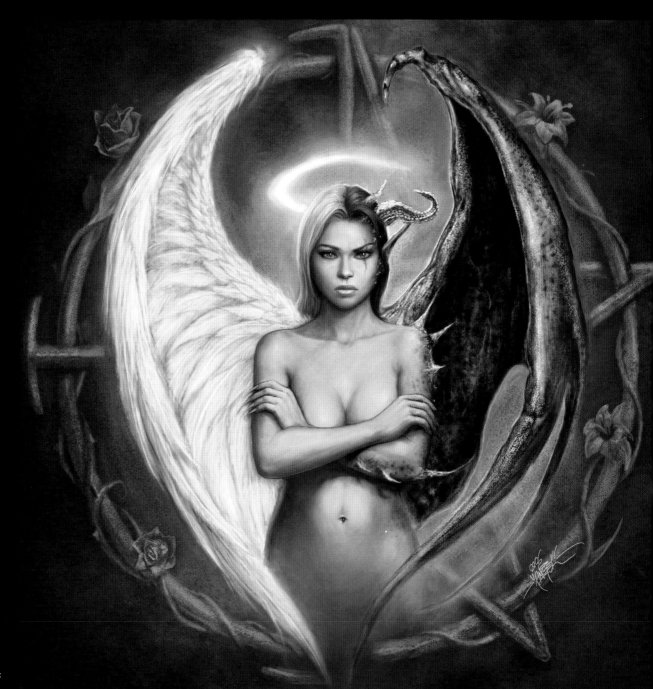

 Divided Heart
Sacha (Angel) Diener
Portfolio piece
Adobe Photoshop
www.angel3d.ch

*Light and dark cannot exist
without each other; no good
without evil; no hope without
suffering. This duality is within
each and every soul, sometimes
conflicting to almost rip you
apart. An eternal fight until the
very last breath you may take; this
is what "Divided Heart" depicts.*

▶ **Melody of Spring**
Kuang Hong
Private commission
Corel Painter
www.zemotion.net

The sultry beauty plucking at the strings of her lyre harks back to classical mythology, yet she's been placed in a truly modern setting. The wistful, transient look on her face speaks of a sadness and loss that can only be imagined.

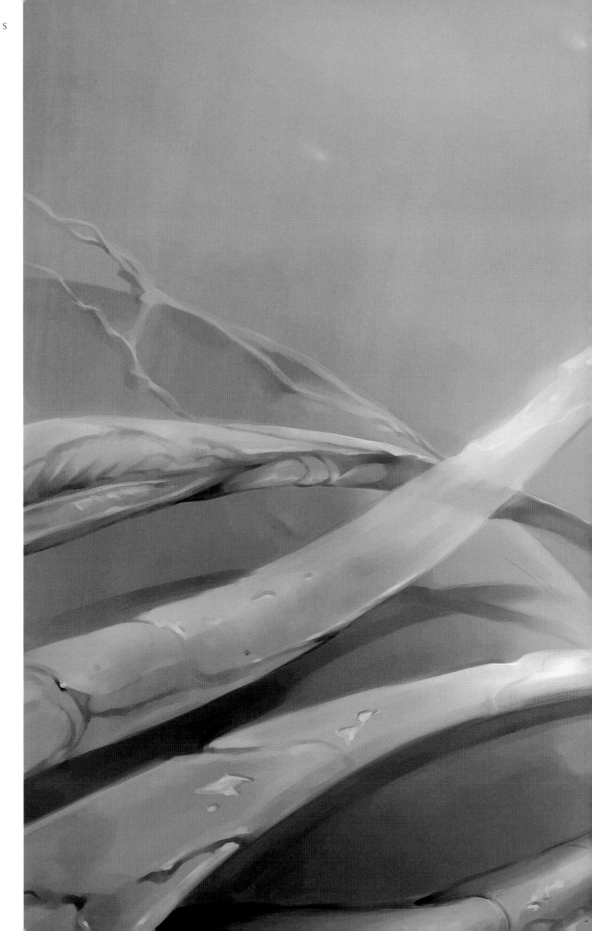

106

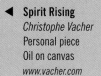 **Fairy**
Christophe Vacher
Portfolio piece
Watercolor on paper
www.vacher.com

This is Christophe providing
us with a personal look into
the world of fairies. The
background of this beautiful
watercolor is inspired by the
area in France where his
parents come. Christophe tells
us that this region has a strong
sense of Celtic history. A simple
composition, with soft greens
and subdued lighting that are
peaceful and relaxing.

◀ **Spirit Rising**
Christophe Vacher
Personal piece
Oil on canvas
www.vacher.com

"I love working with light and
drapes, and I think this is a
good example. The background
has been modeled (loosely) on
mountains in Colorado." The
lighting here is amazing, glowing
through the wonderfully executed
cloth. The eagle seems to present a
shamanistic element to the picture.

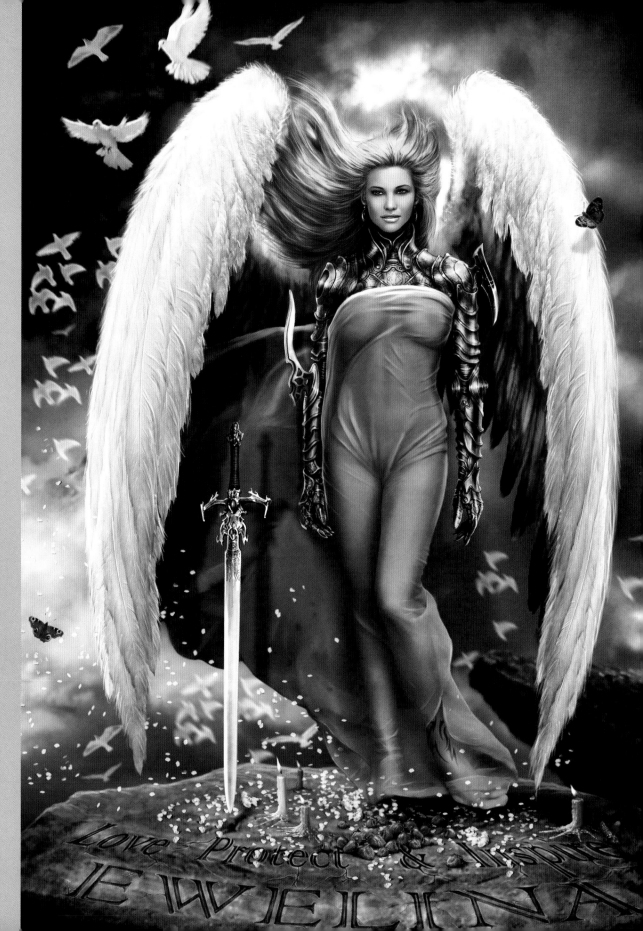

◀ **Ina's Angel**
Tariq Raheem
Portfolio piece
Digital media
www.tariqart.com

*Where would fantasy art be
without angels? This striking
woman is a fine example from
Tariq. Flying is a central theme
to this image, with birds and
butterflies complementing the
wings of the angel. Is there
some sort of symbolism in the
strawberries? Perhaps we are
left to decide…*

▶ **Angels**
Kareem Ettouney
Portfolio piece
Acrylic and Adobe Photoshop
www.kareemettouney.com

*In this abstract piece, Kareem
portrays the characters
intertwining and twisting
around each other to seemingly
form one body. The angels and
the demons blend in a way that
could be seen as symbolic if it
weren't for the thoroughly
erotic nature of their bonding.*

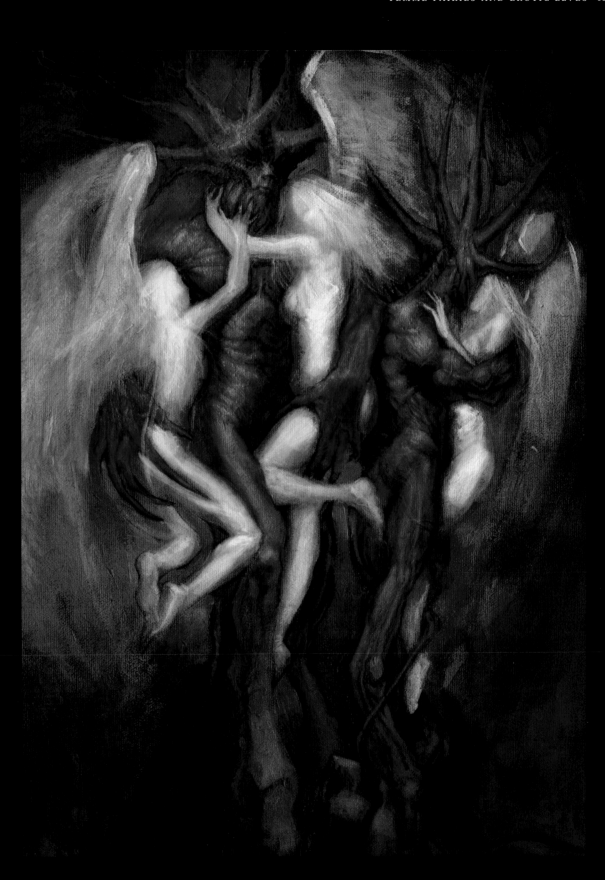

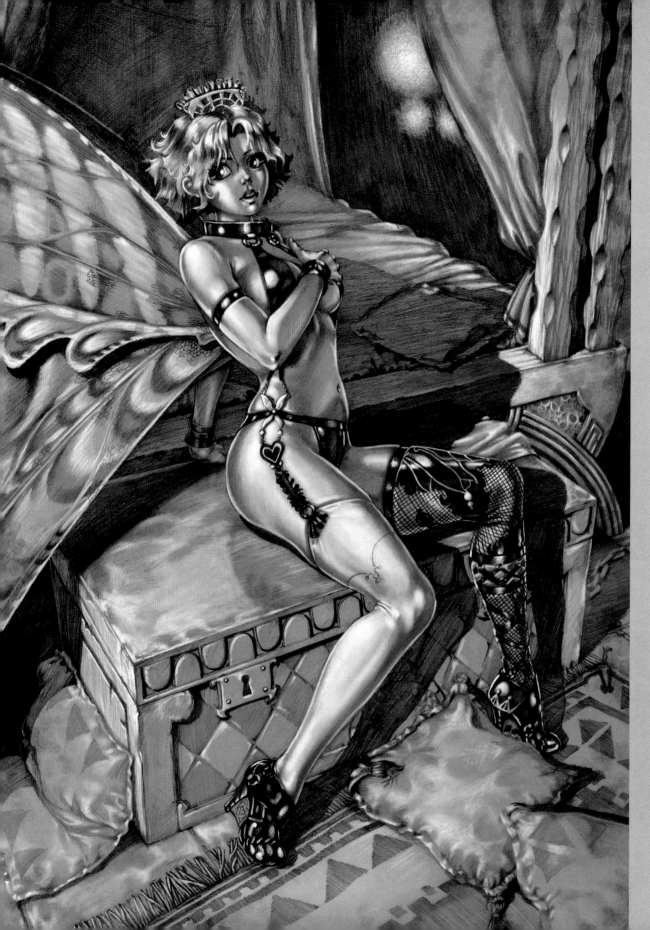

Holly Temptation
Andy Hepworth
Portfolio piece
Painter IX.5 and pencil
www.andyhepworth.com

I'd wanted to do a real pin-up for some time, and waited until I finally found the space in my schedule to complete this image. It was a real labor to pencil the A2 image, and then scan it for toning using an A4 scanner… Still, it was a nice labor to have had!

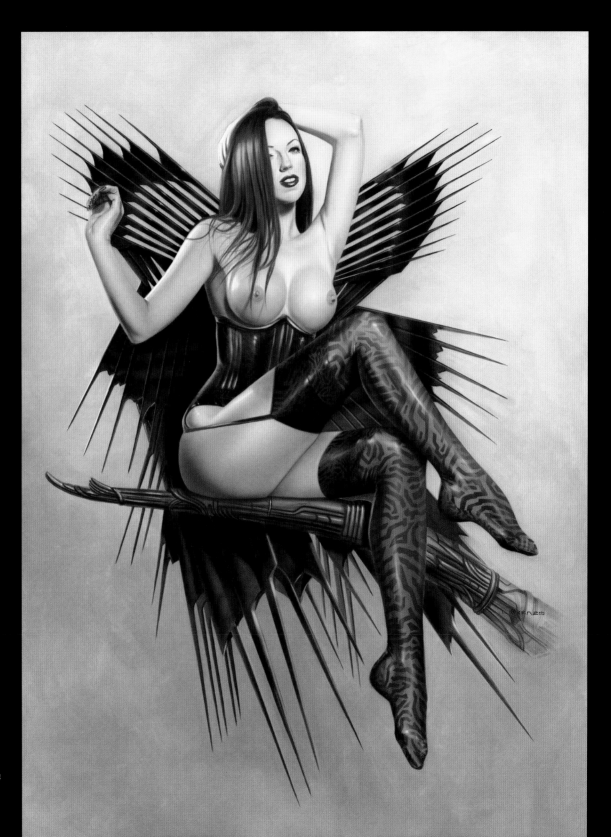

Absynthe
Lorenzo Sperlonga
Portfolio piece
Acrylic
www.lorenzosperlonga.com

Lorenzo has taken the classic approach of the great pin-up artists and brought them up to date in his sexy images. This is reflected in the use of stockings and suspenders so commonly seen in the work of artists like Gil Elvgren, although it's been given a new twist here. In "Absynthe," the character's wing design is just one of the strong elements of originality on display

▶ **Art Nouveau II**
Daniela Uhlig
Portfolio piece
Adobe Photoshop
www.du-artwork.de

This painting is part of a series by Daniela inspired by the Art Nouveau movement. She tells us "It was very important for me that this painting matched the others, so I used a similar color palette. Also I wanted to show different girls; here a blonde."

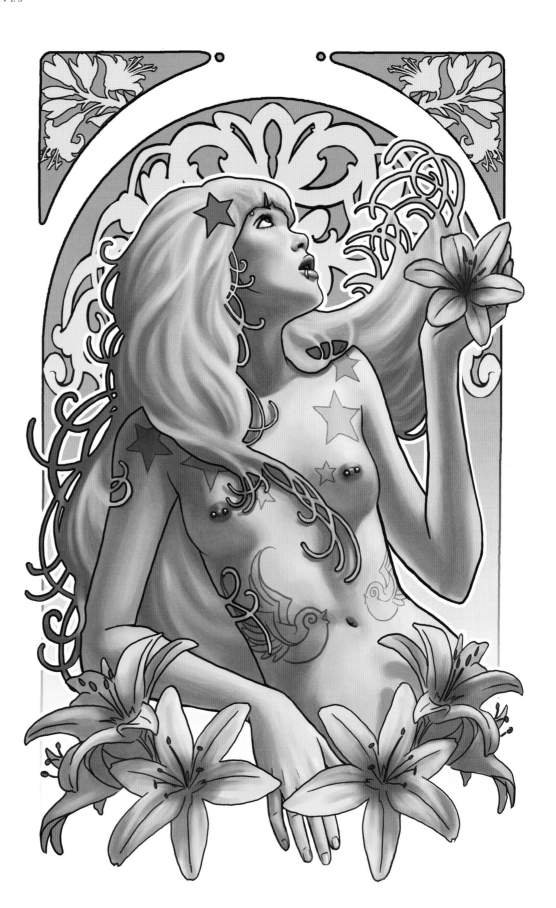

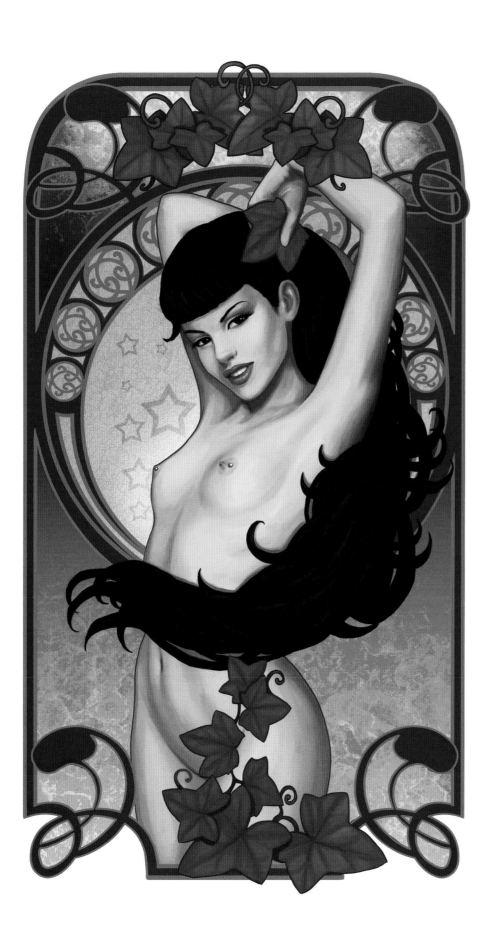

◀ **Art Nouveau III**
Daniela Uhlig
Portfolio piece
Photoshop CS2
www.du-artwork.de

In the third painting in her Art Nouveau series, Daniela informs us: "The girl in this painting is a brunette, and a classic pin-up character." Daniela intends to create a further nine Art Nouveau images for a calendar to be produced in the future.

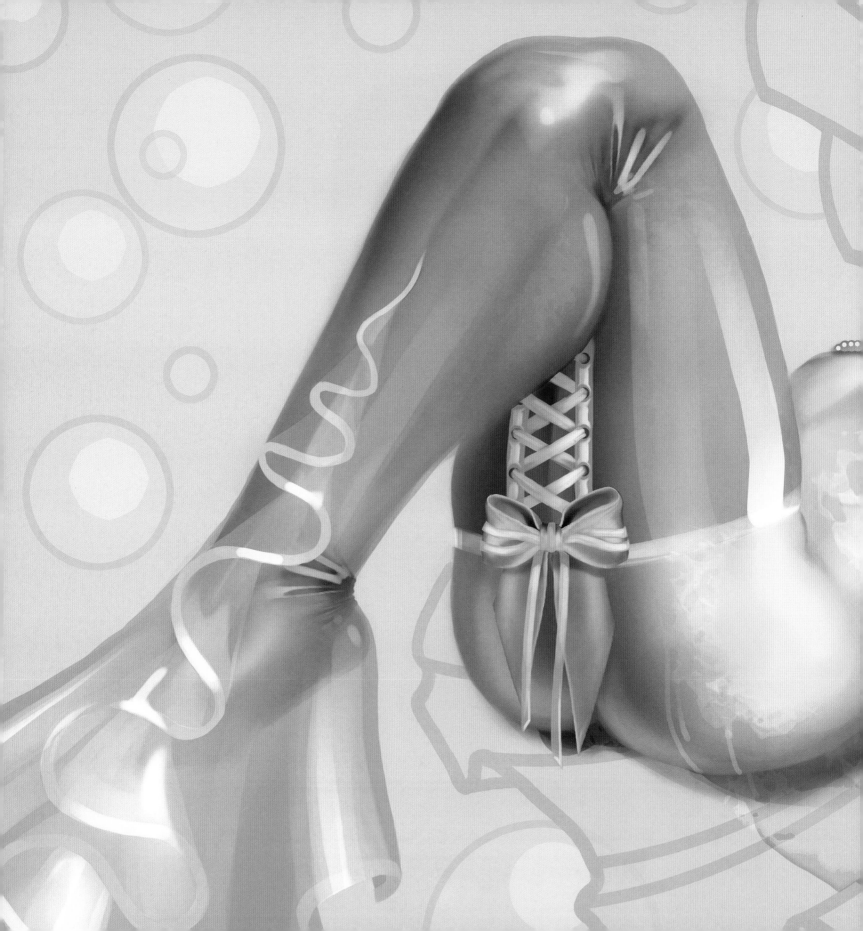

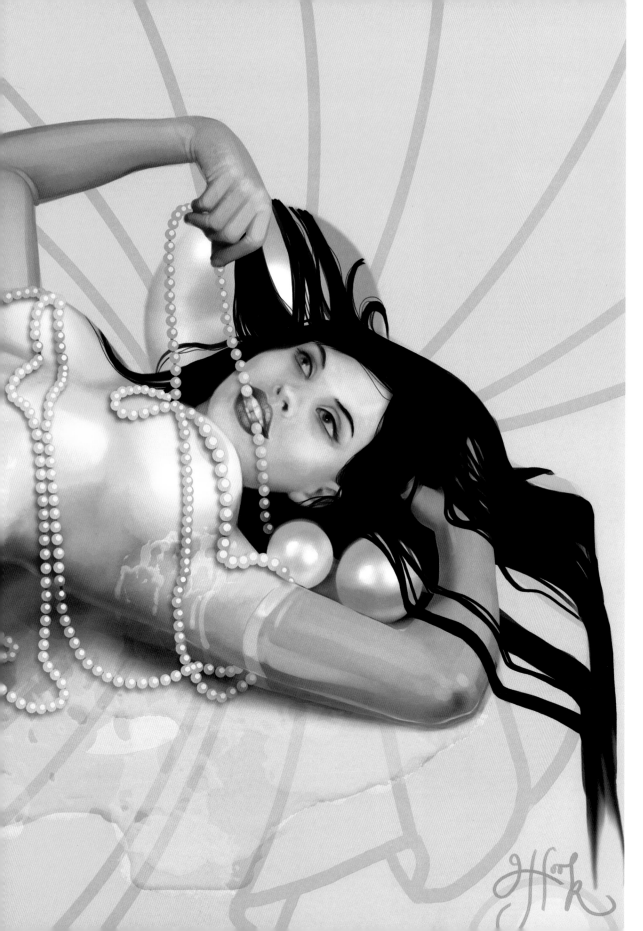

Mermaid
Jessica Hook
Portfolio piece
Adobe Photoshop
www.JessicaHook.com
www.ConceptArt.org

I painted this mermaid piece specifically for this book. As soon as I saw the book's title, the cogs in my head started turning in the most delectable way. I knew I wanted to make something naughty, and I kept coming up with sordid innuendos... some a little more morally debased than others! So I narrowed it down a bit, and in the end a few choice ideas came together like pearls on a string.

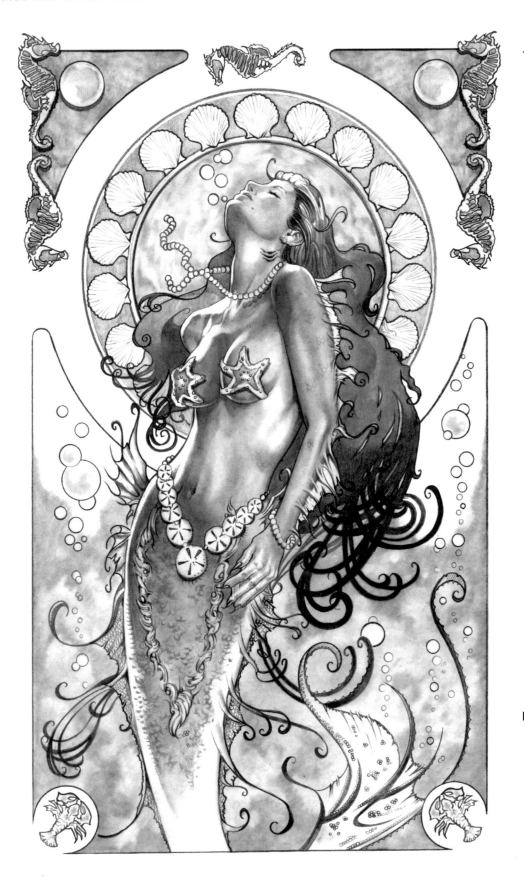

◀ **Mermaiden**
Tom Fleming
Self-published limited edition
print of 600
Pencil
www.flemart.com

*A Mucha-inspired picture from
Tom. The mermaid breaks up
the geometric shapes of the
background without detracting
from the overall design; a feature
commonly seen in Mucha's work,
and emulated skilfully here.*

▶ **Anjo Do Mal (Dark Angel)**
Steve Sampson
Portfolio piece
Adobe Photoshop and Illustrator
www.sampsonart.com

*In this image I wanted to
continue mixing my love of
graphic design with a more
traditional painting style.*

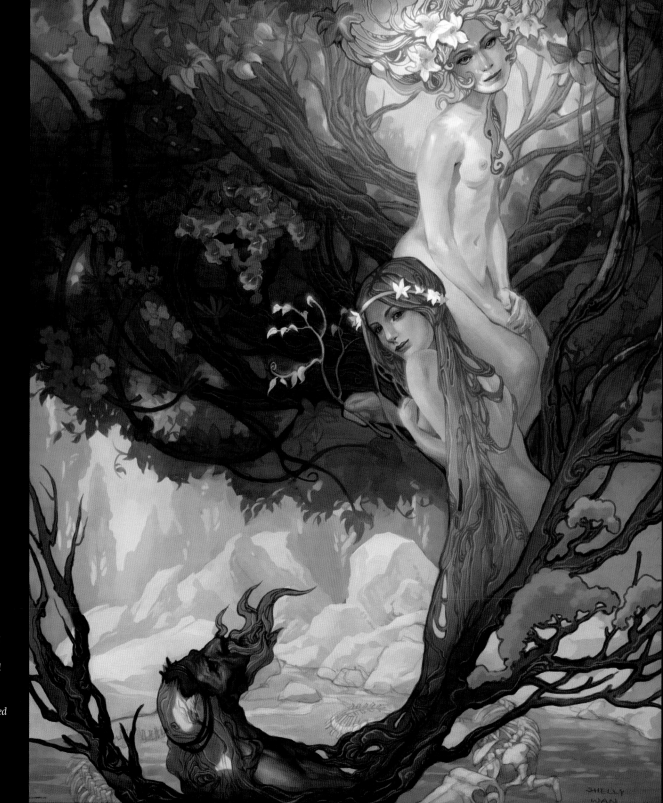

Lance and Gwen
Johann de Venecia
Portfolio piece
Adobe Photoshop

My version of Lancelot and Guinevere from the Arthurian legend. I used a loose, sketchy feel, to give their impassioned meeting some energy.

Spring
Shelly Wan
Pin-up calendar submission for CA.org *Chicks who draw chicks*
Adobe Photoshop, Corel Painter and pencil
shellywan.blogspot.com

CA.org's girls organized a fun project that we can do together: a Pin-up calendar. I chose "Spring" as the season I wanted to create for the calendar as it contains the Life/Death motif that I am drawn to. So I pictured a flower bud, blossoming from bones — young from old — and from those words I have the image of the young nymphs gracefully emerging through Old Man Winter's chest.

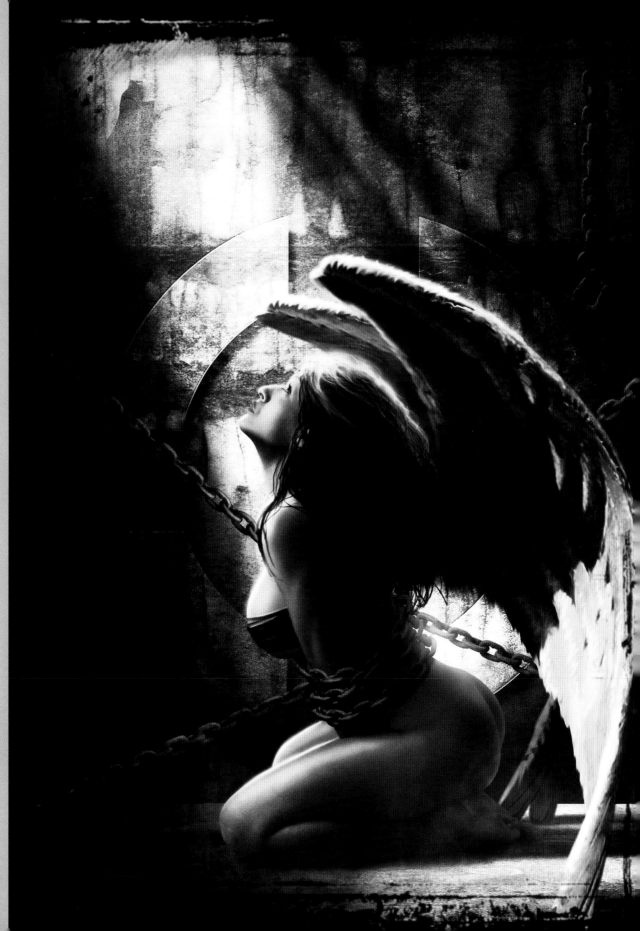

◄ Seraph
Patrick J. Jones
Portfolio piece
Oil and Corel Painter
www.pjartworks.com

Sometimes, too many commissions are hanging in the air to risk taking on another job while waiting for go-aheads. This is a good time to work on a private piece, which keeps me busy and helps me keep the rust at bay. Painting fantasy without outside art direction or literary constraints is about as good as it gets. In an ideal world I'd paint picture after picture for myself, compile them into fantasy art books and calendars every two years, and swan around waving to international applause...

► The Light
Tony Mauro
Portfolio piece
Adobe Photoshop
www.darkdayproductions.com

"The Light" was challenging because I've wanted to do an angel piece for a while, but wasn't sure how to make it fit into my dark style. It's not like me to have a glowing angel sitting on a puffy cloud in a perfect blue sky, so I had to come up with a concept that featured an angel, but still had the mood and feeling that people expect from my work. I am very happy with the result, and love the implication of an imprisoned angel locked in some sort of underground vault, with a single beam of hope breaking into her space. The model was Christine, a good friend of mine.

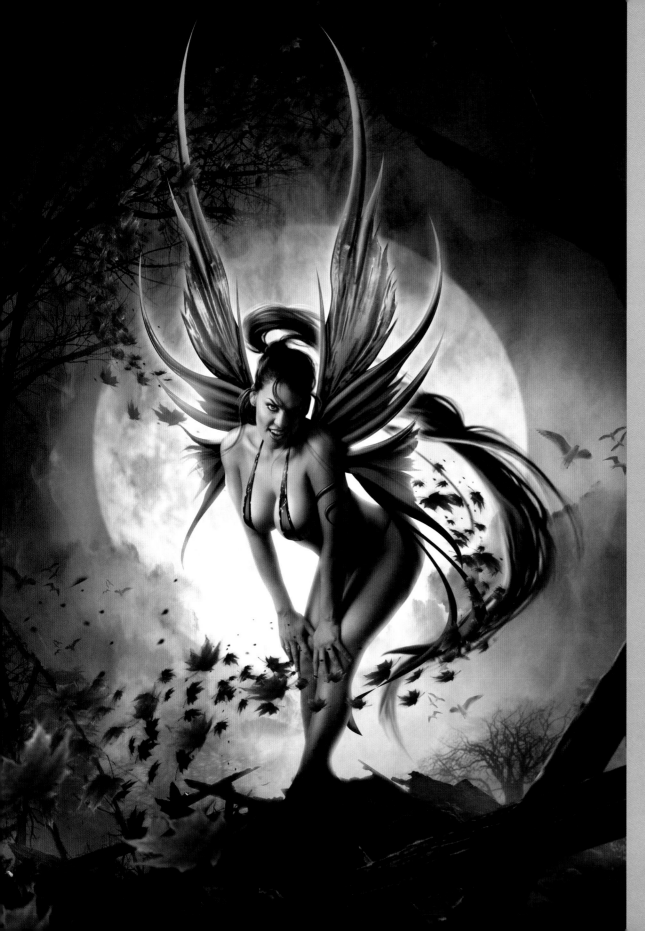

◄ **O'Lovely Fairy**
Tony Mauro
Portfolio piece
Tony Mauro Merchandise
Digital, Photoshop
www.darkdayproductions.com

This piece was my first opportunity to work with the beautiful Olivia O'Lovely, who has quite a following in the adult film industry. When I met her at a pin-up convention in Los Angeles, where we were both exhibiting, I jumped on the opportunity to work with her. She is a big fairy fan with several fairy tattoos on her body. When the question "What do you want to be in your piece?" came up, you don't have to waste too many guesses on what her answer was.

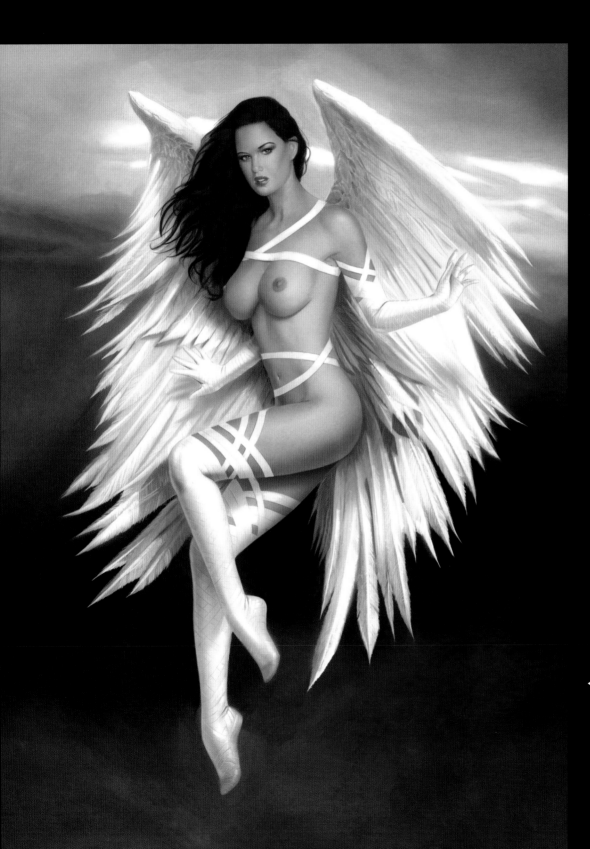

◄ **White Angel**
Lorenzo Sperlonga
Portfolio piece
Acrylic
www.lorenzosperlonga.com

*Angels are always popular with
fantasy pin-up artists, and
this is another fine example
from Lorenzo. Her expression is
completely unself aware, and, as
a result, even more appealing.*

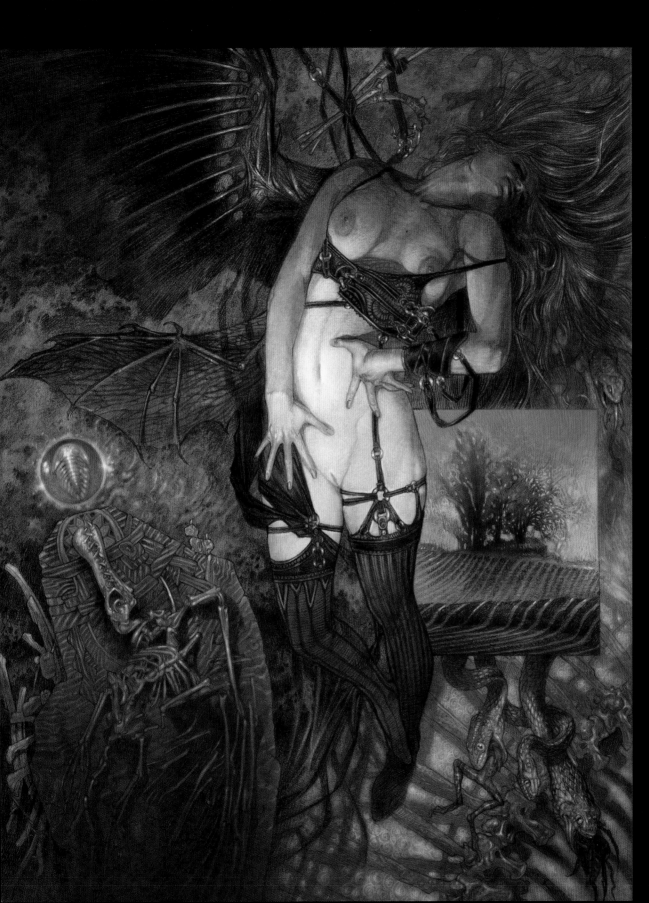

◀ **E2 Metis**
Mark Nelson
Portfolio piece
Pencil and Adobe Photoshop
www.*GrazingDinosaurPress.com*

*This is a hybrid of two series
that I have been working on. The
first series was called "Broken
Angels" and the other deals with
"Medusa and Metis". With the
research I've done into old-world
symbols, Metis was the Greek
word for female knowledge, and
the Medusa was also thought of
as the Goddess of life and death.*

▶ **Sacred Hour II**
Christophe Vacher
Personal piece
Oil on canvas
www.*vacher.com*

*Christophe tells us that this is one
of his only paintings that hasn't
sold yet, although it's still very
popular. A beautifully lit and
rendered image, the golden hues
give it a warmth and intensity
which are emphasized by the
strong lighting that draws us to
the center of the composition.*

Angel Study
Eric Bailey
Portfolio piece
Oil on canvas
www.birdsandbullets.com

San Francisco artist Eric Bailey
has a vigorous painting style
that produces canvasses thick
with paint. The subject of
"Angel Study" gazes at the sky,
enveloped by her dark wings
and a swinging crucifix. The
low viewing angle adds further
interest and frustrates the viewer
by hiding the angel's face, and
ultimately her thoughts.

▶ **Angelica**
Les Toil
Private commission
Pen and ink, digitally colored

For every racy and provocative
erotic dream, most of us have
fantasies colored in purity
and innocence that are no
less arousing. What could be
more ethereal than a beautiful,
curvaceous, and elusive being
showing pleasures unknown
to mortal imagination in a
far-off mythic utopia? The wings
suggest that if you can capture
her, she's yours... for as long as
you can keep her satisfied.

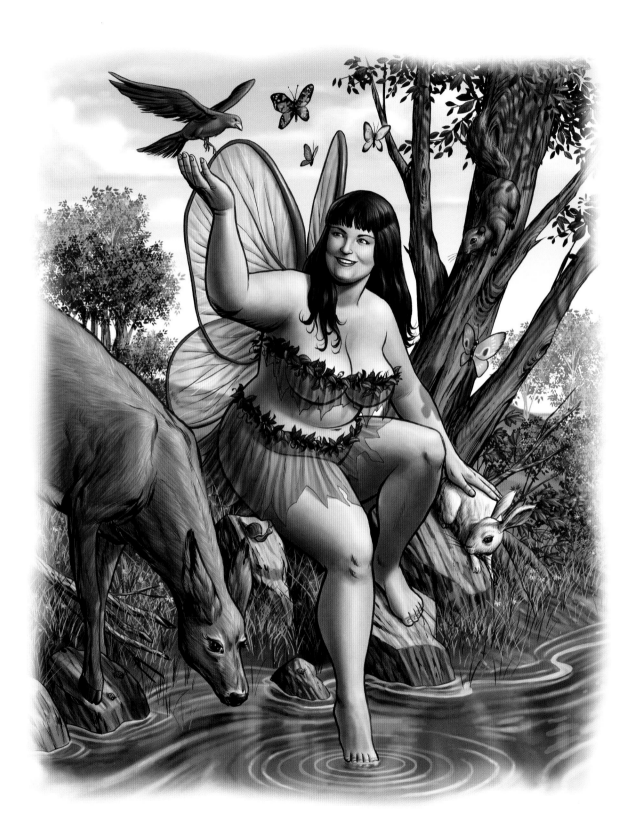

▶ **Spring**
Tom Fleming
Self-published limited edition
print of 500
Pencil
www.flemart.com

*With Mucha-esque elements
and design, this beautiful
representation of "Spring"
personified is a wistful and
romanticized image. Around
the girl are hummingbirds,
butterflies, and bees, along
with various plants to describe
the season. A strong image,
presented in black and white
as part of a series of the four
seasons from this artist.*

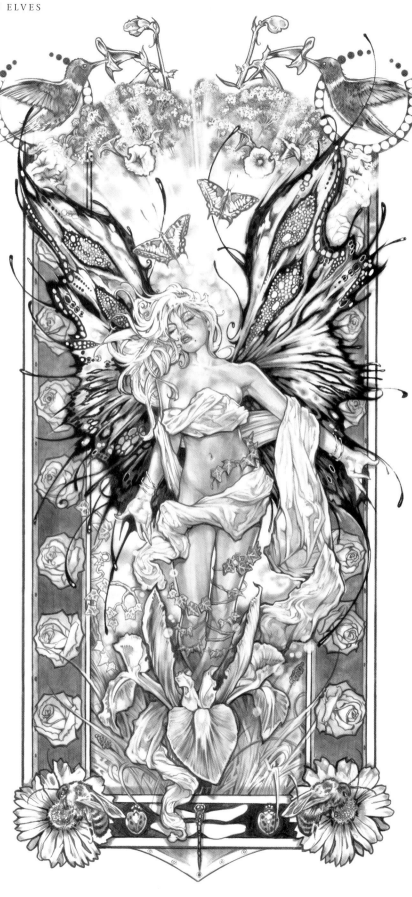

▶ **Victory Gal Angel of Death**
Glen Angus
Portfolio piece
Adobe Photoshop
www.gangus.net

*This painting was done as part
of my "Victory Gals" body of
work. This is one of the more
gruesome paintings for this
series (hopefully to be picked
up as a calendar). It shows the
purest version of death and
destruction from that time, in
the depiction of the Gal on the
"Fatman" bomb dropped over
Japan. It is done with a cruel
and blunt approach, to portray
beauty in such a horrific thing.*

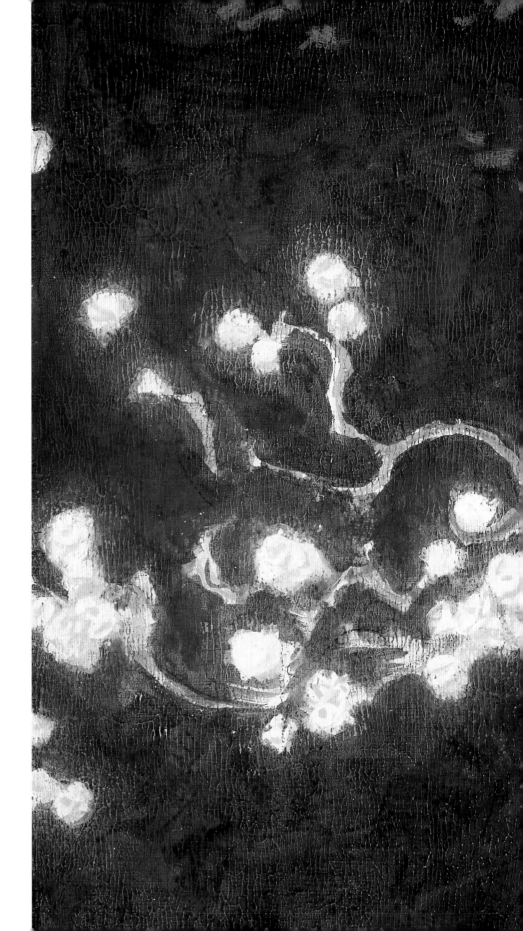

 Flower Expanse
Craig Elliot
Portfolio piece
Acrylic, pastel, and oil
www.craigelliotgallery.com

*A study in the power of Mother
Nature to grow out from a source
and take over again, despite any
assault we, or other forces make
upon her.*

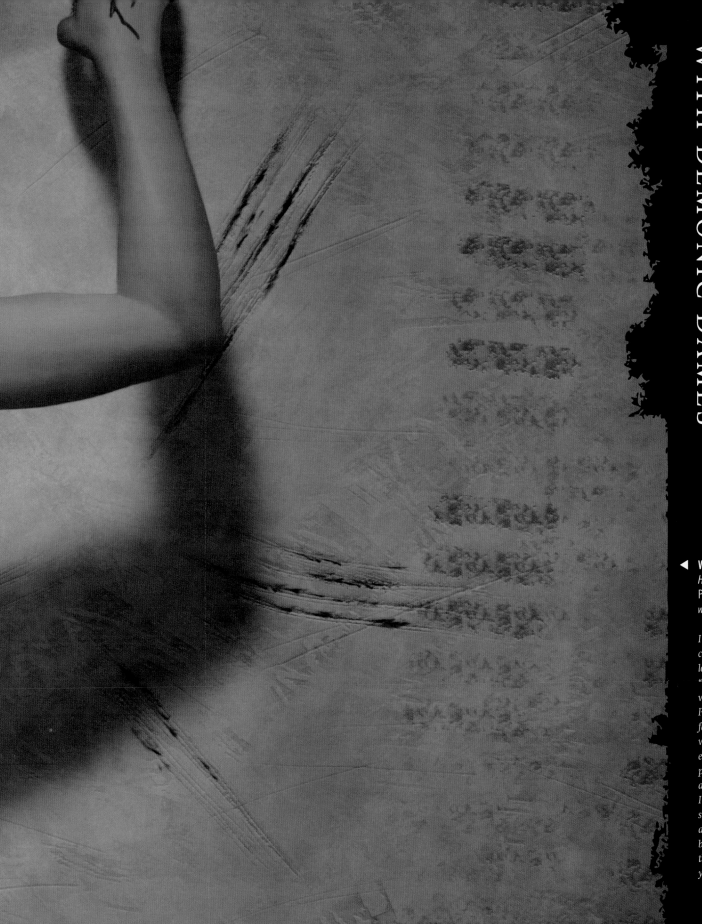

CHAPTER 5
DANGEROUS LIAISONS
WITH DEMONIC DAMES

◀ **Wall**
Henning Ludvigsen
Portfolio piece
www.henningludvigsen.com

*I rarely have ideas for painting
cooking inside my head for a
long time, but due to limited tin
"Wall" had to wait for almost a
whole year before being realized
Personally, I enjoy painting
fantasy-related imagery, often
with somewhat odd or skewed
elements to it. But I wanted this
piece to be more serious and
artistic than my usual work.
I wanted the girl to appear
strong and erotic, but still have
a disturbing side to her. The
background should be simple an
the skin tones cold and complex
yet appearing monochromatic.*

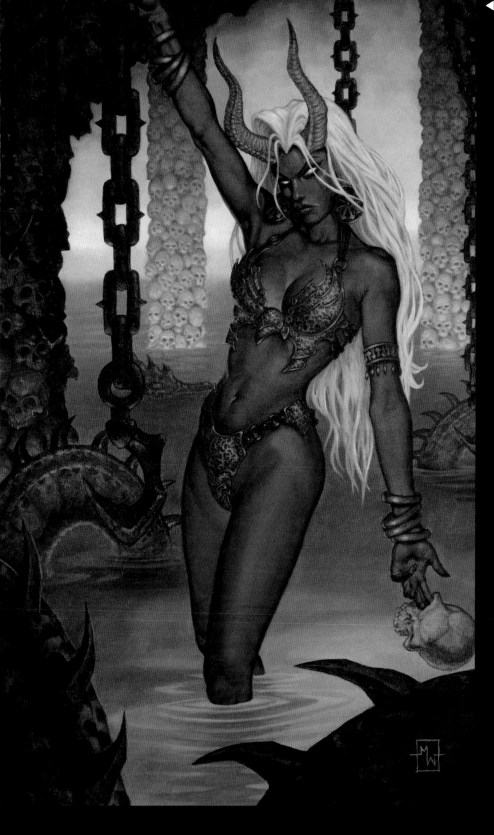

Chains
Matt Wilson
Illustration: *Magic the Gathering*
Oil on board
www.mattwilsonart.com

In 1997 my work was getting censored left and right on these cards, so this is a great example of how things have changed. The "Chains" painting got through the review process without even raising an eyebrow, yet six years before I brought things to a screeching halt with a pair of white briefs! Nowadays, naked fat guys in bondage don't even show up on the radar. That's what I call progress!

Lady Demon
Matt Wilson
Chaos Comics Swimsuit
Spectacular Art Compilation
Oil on board
www.mattwilsonart.com

Fantasy art is about being bigger than life, but I'm not a big fan of women in metal bikinis squatting on mountain-tops licking their swords—unless there's good reason for it. The Lady Demon piece was an opportunity to indulge any urges to do a cheesecake pin-up and remain completely guilt free. It's like eating dessert and not gaining any weight.

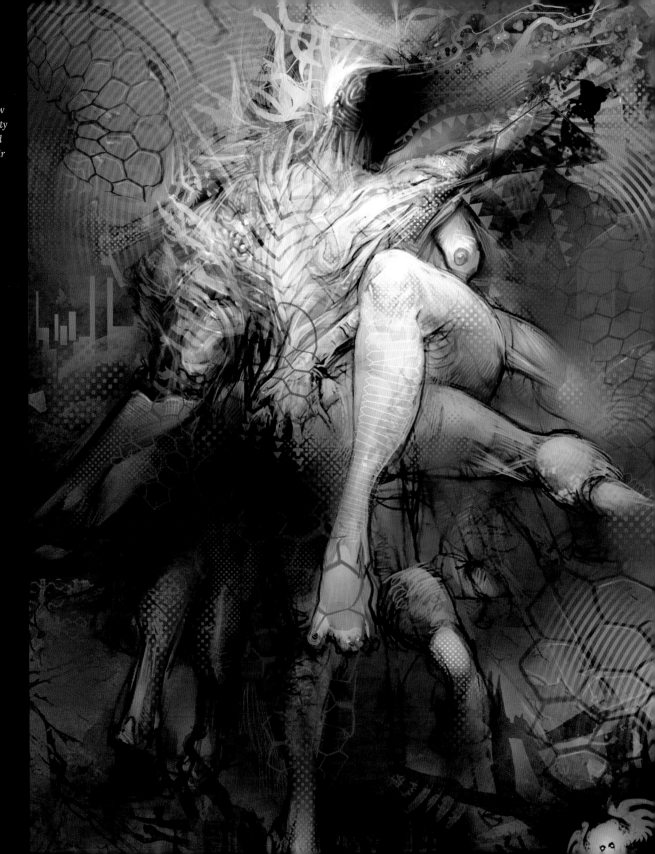

ire Fight Fuck

Andrew Jones

Flyer illustration

Corel Painter

www.androidjones.com

Before I moved from Austin to San Francisco I decided to throw one last massive party. The party was also an erotic art show and this was the flyer I created to stir up interest for the Texas tribe.

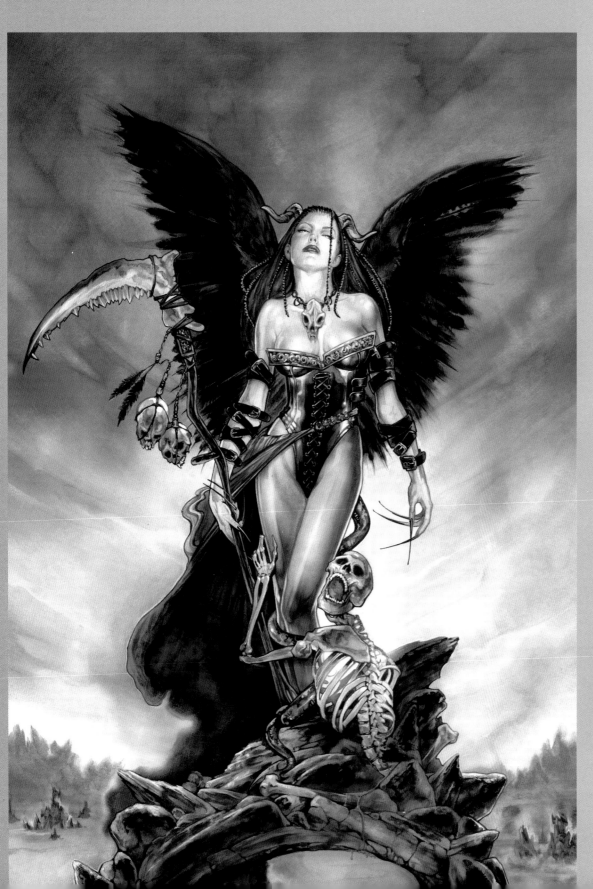

◄ **Soul Harvest**
Tom Fleming
Self-published limited
edition print of 1,000
Watercolor, color pencil,
and acrylic
www.flemart.com

*"Soul Harvest" seems to depict
the Angel of Death, with her
scythe and beautifully rendered
wings. At her feet, a skeletal
corpse clings with a desperate
longing. Tom skilfully uses
watercolor to present this black
angel and the palette is subdued,
as befits the theme.*

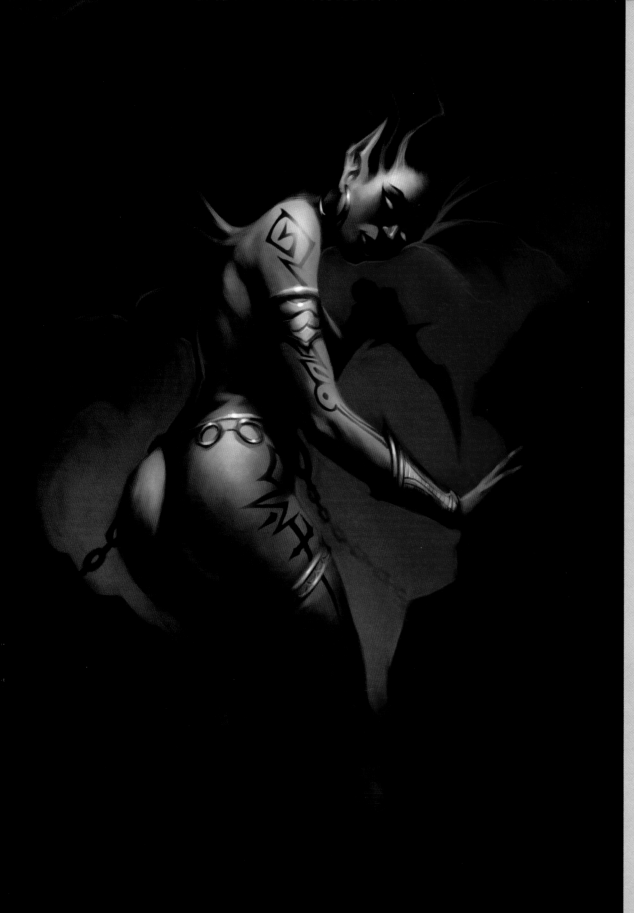

◀ **Demona**
Patrick Reilly
Portfolio piece
Digital media: Adobe Photoshop,
Corel Painter
http://preilly.deviantart.com/gallery

*I used to love browsing through
the vintage fantasy art that
graced the covers of many
novels in the 1970s. I thought
it might be fun to pay homage,
by creating a piece that evoked
the feel of those great-old "sword
and sorcery" style paintings.*

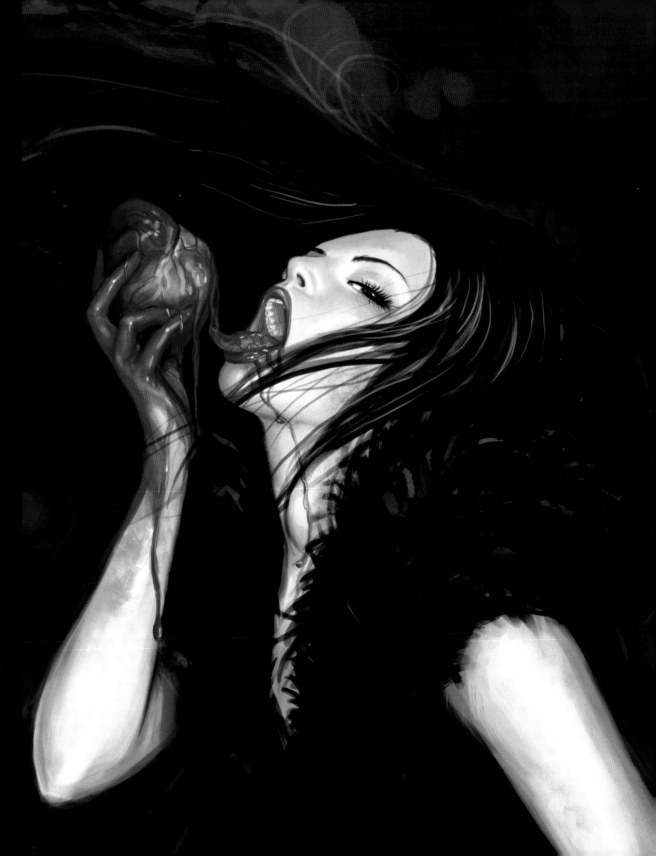

▶ **Queen of Hearts**
Daniela Uhlig
Personal piece
Adobe Photoshop
www.du-artwork.de

The "Queen of Hearts" is a two- to three-hour speedpainting inspired by Elizabeth Báthory, the true-life, Hungarian-born "Vampire Queen", also known as the Blood Countess. During the late 16th century, Báthory is supposed to have killed more than 600 young women and bathed in their blood in the vain attempt to retain her youth.

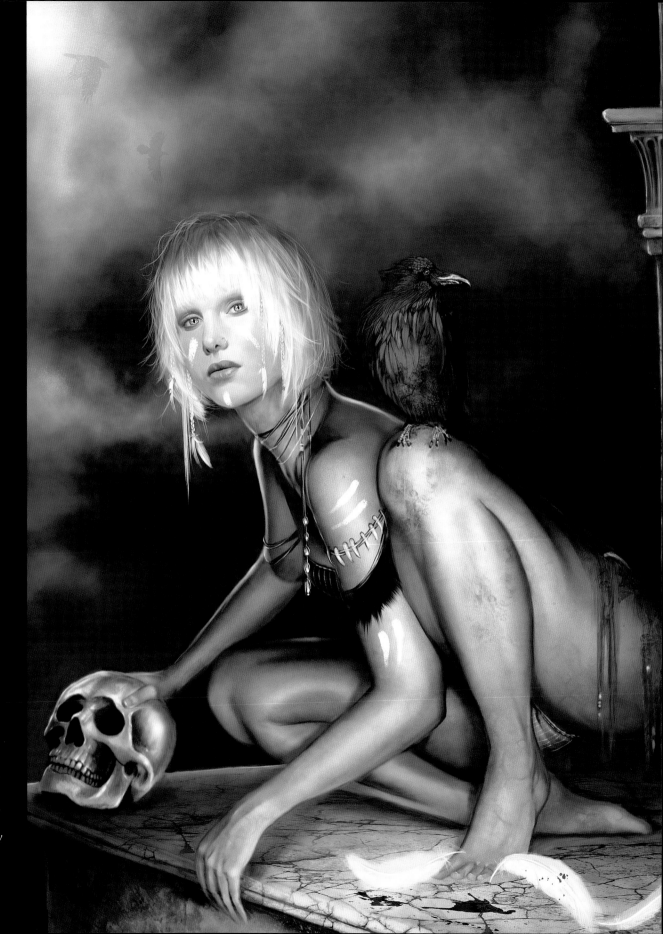

Vampyre Planet
Patrick J Jones
Portfolio piece
Oil and Corel Painter
www.pjartworks.com

This is a new painting using a figure from an older work. I thought the figure was promising, but suited a better idea, so I almost entirely repainted her, removing most of her oufit and adding a new background. I liked the idea of setting her against the background of a "Vampyre Planet". Her flaming hair evolved as the painting progressed, as did the tail, which doubled as an aesthetic device to break up the diagonals in the picture. As usual, the struggle here was to hold back on superfluous detail.

The Soul Collector
Natascha Roeoesli
Portfolio piece
Adobe Photoshop
www.tascha.ch

Painting skin and muscle structure was a new challenge for me. The idea was to create a dark-themed, slightly tribal-inspired nude female. Once more, the idea was to make her look seductive, with a hint of danger and a mystical aura. In general I prefer darker themes, even though I am quite a cheery person in real life. I guess it is some kind of balance I need in my work.

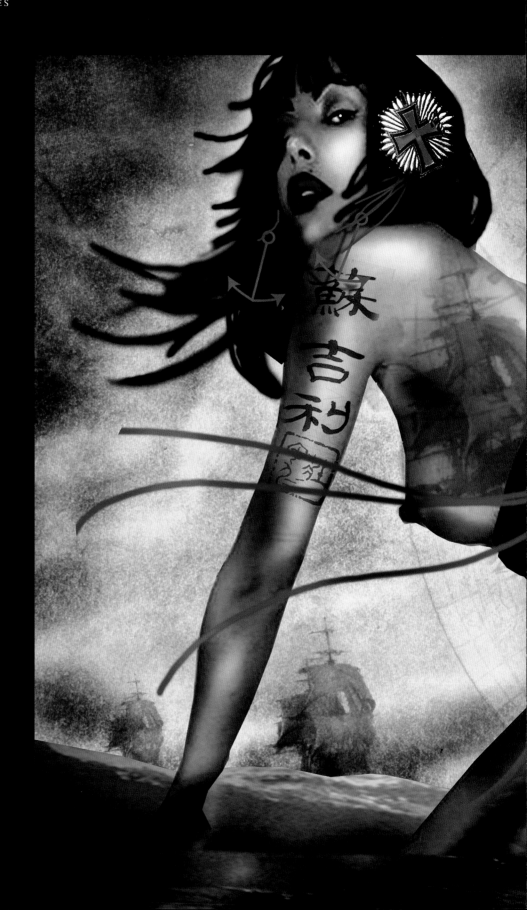

▶ **Buoy Four**
Chris Spollen
Self-published in Art Zine
Digital media
www.spollen.com

This image goes back to my adolescent years, when I would journey out into my local harbor. Here, I commanded a small twelve-foot rowboat with a recycled outboard motor. I would drift along the channel, baking in the summer's heat, while fantasizing about Spanish ships and pirate women. As I get older, I find myself going back to these moments more and more.

▶ **Love Lies Dying**
Vince Natale
Book cover: *Love Lies Dying*
Bloodletting Press
Oil
www.vincenatale.com

*This was used as a book jacket
for a limited-edition collector's
version of a horror/psychological
thriller book entitiled Love
Lies Dying by the Australian
author Steve Gerlach. The
figure pictured — Zoe — is the
protagonist of this story, about
a psychotic woman who kills an
old acquaintance's wife and then
tricks him into going to an old
stone church. She then ties him to
a table and performs some S&M
activities in order to make him
submit to her.*

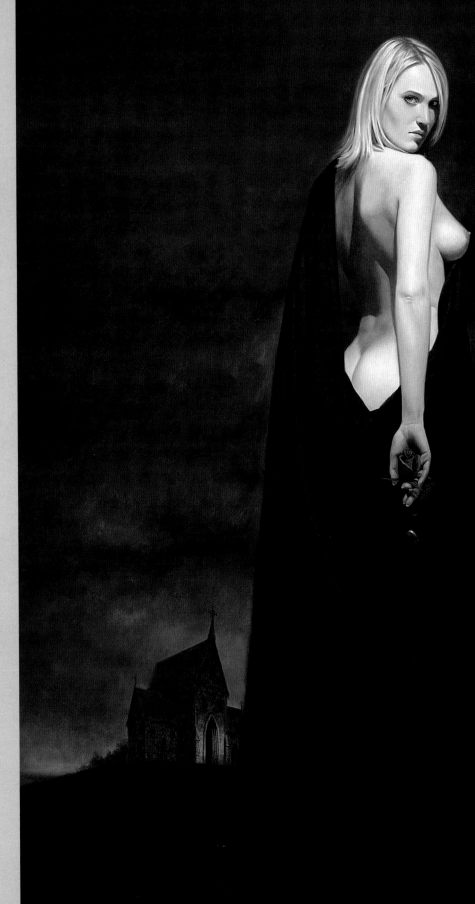

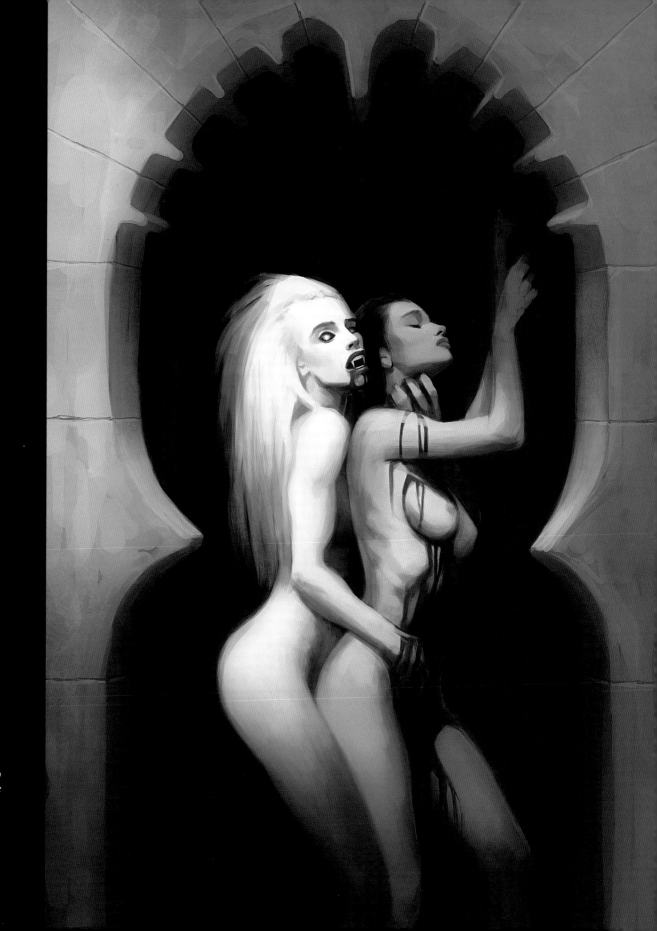

Willing Victim
Christian Bravery
Portfolio piece
Adobe Photoshop
www.leadinglightdesign.com

A thoroughly erotic lesbian
vampire image, harking back to
the classics of cinematic vampire
movies such as "Twins of Evil"
and "The Vampire Lovers". The
vampire in this picture appears
to have been caught in the act
as she glances at us. A personal
study, used as a portfolio piece.

◄ **Death and its Brides**
Loic (e338) Zimmermann
Portfolio piece
Digital media
www.e338.com

In this dark piece, created specifically for this book, Loic presents his vision of Death, flanked, and embraced, by his brides. He wrote a poem to accompany his piece, which we felt was a little too steamy to translate!

Oh ça oui !
Les deux petites cherchaient des sensations.
Et c'est un fait qu'IL leur en donnerait.
Et puis même qu' IL les baiserait!
Jusqu'à ce qu'elles en perdent la raison.
Mais un peu plus bas dans la vallée,
Où leurs lits étaient encore nostalgiques et chauds,
Et où le courage faisait bien trop souvent défaut,
Papa les pleurait...
La morve au bout du nez.

► **Indigestion**
R.K. Post
Commission
www.rkpost.net
© Wizards of the Coast Digital media

This picture was produced to reflect a compendium of alien creatures for a now-defunct role-playing game. I thought that giving her a deadpan look — as she was about to die — was perfect to illustrate the defiance that one can have against insurmountable odds.

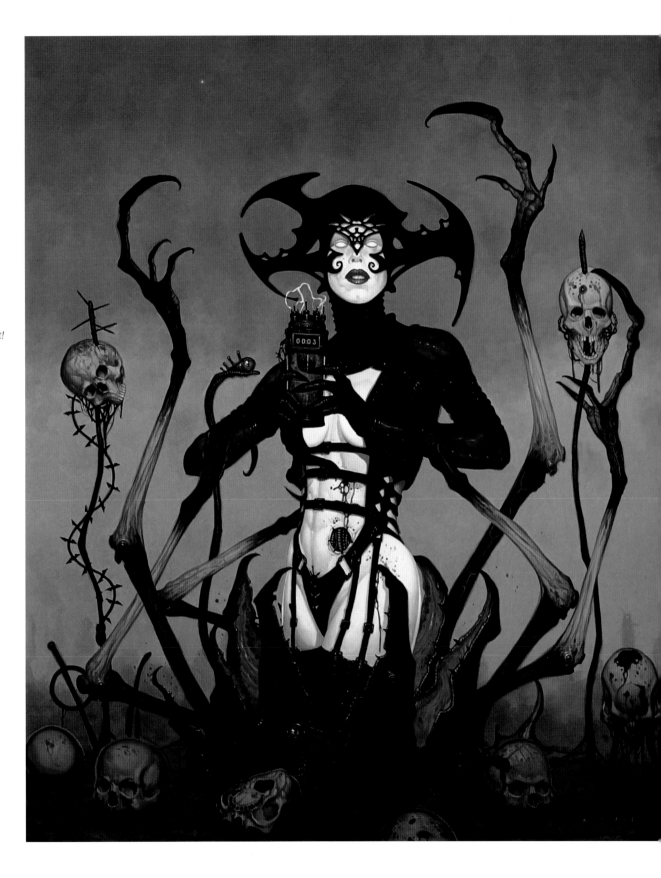

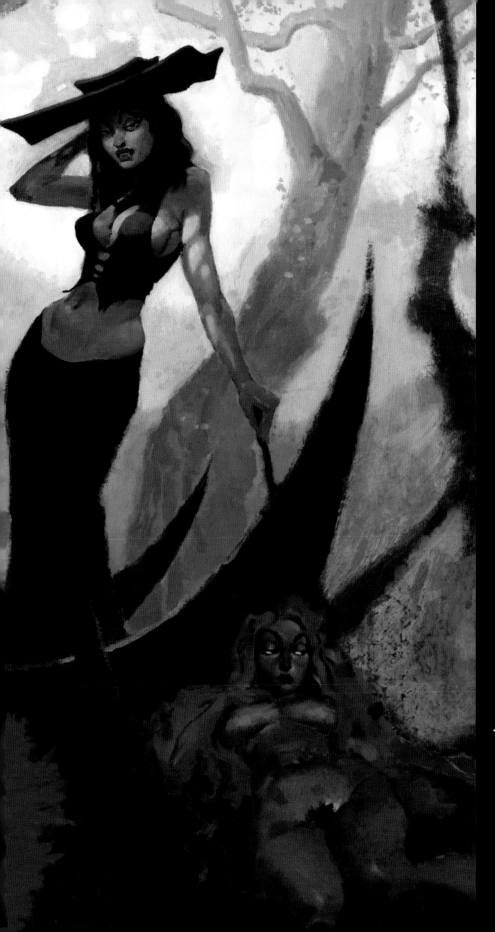

◀ **Vampiresses Fishing**
Craig Elliot
Portfolio work
Oil over acrylic
www.craigelliotgallery.com

*A vampiress and her court
of minions on a fishing and
bathing outing to the swamp...
Is it more or less moral to be
a parasite?*

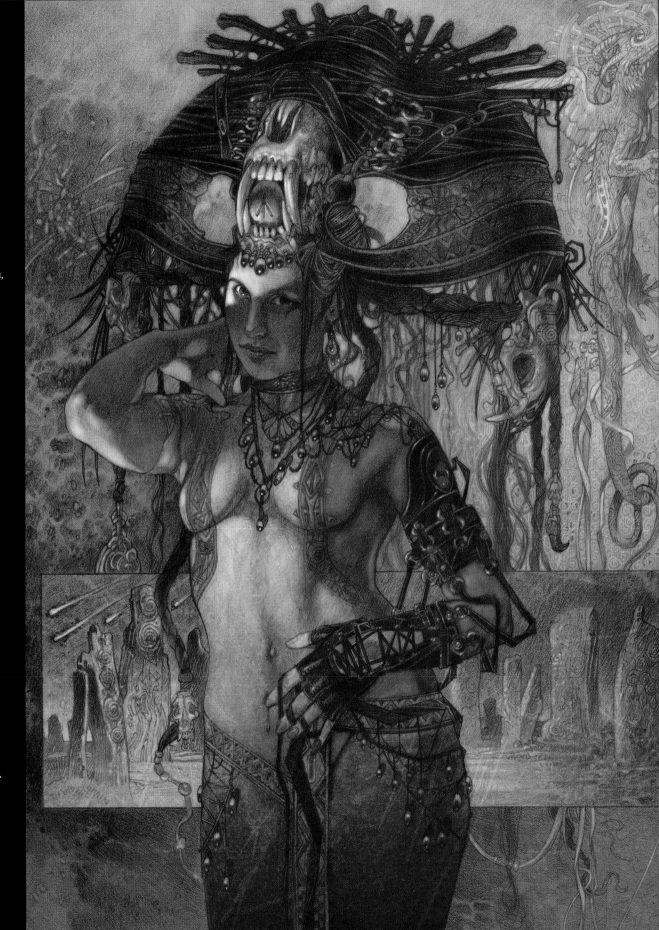

Blue Dream
Nestor Taylor
Client: Hot Valencia
Acrylic and airbrush

Created for Hot Valencia in Spain, the idea incorporates a bat—which is a Valencian icon—into an image that fits the theme required by the client. This is a lady who likes to coordinate her clothing with her soft furnishings, and there is no ambiguity in the bare flesh, blatant eroticism and the sultry gaze behind the mask.

RR Morganna
Mark Nelson
Portfolio piece
Pencil and Adobe Photoshop
www.GrazingDinosaurPress.com

The runic symbol "Yr" in the headdress has been manipulated to become a symbol of the World Tree, Yggdrasil, and the entrance to the Underworld. Other contemporary thoughts include femaleness, night, and the opposite of the man rune. The model has a celtic background and her animal sign is the fire dragon.

▶ **Hope 13**
Kino Siablabba
Portfolio piece
Digital media
www. homepage.mac.com/kinoo/
PhotoAlbum4.html

*Kino's fantastic use of design
in this image presents us
with a dark, unforgiving
image, almost at odds with
its optimistic title. Shadowy
figures lurk around the central
character, who occupies a
dominant presence in the
picture, her head haloed by
esoteric symbols.*

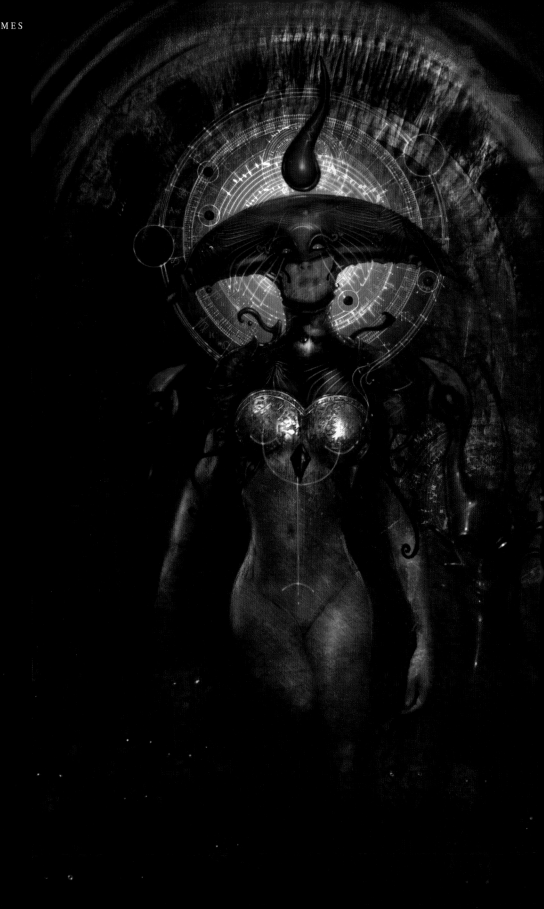

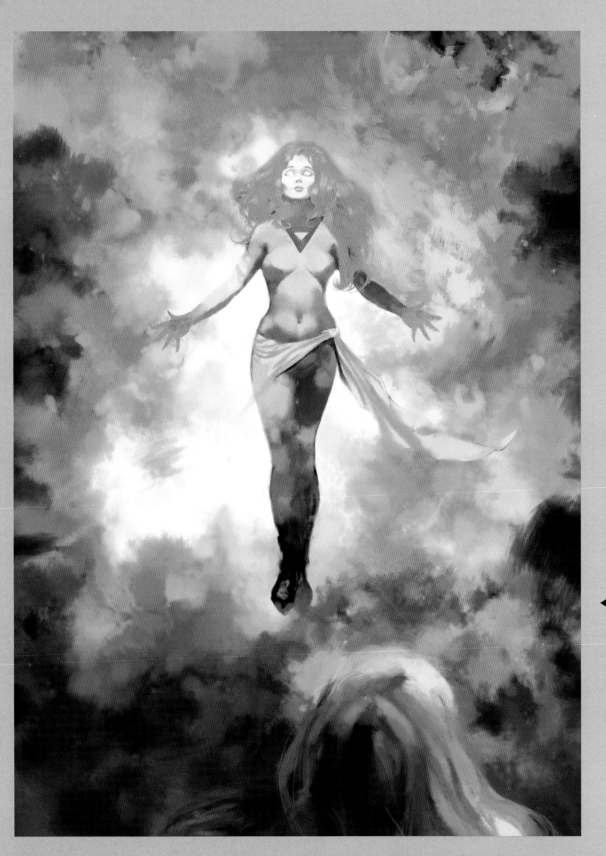

◄ **Phoenix**
Arthur Suydam
Commision: X-Men
Traditional media
www.arthursuydam.com

*Arthur's depiction of the X-Men
character "Phoenix", represented
in the form of Jean Grey in all its
fiery glory. A dramatic image,
with enormous energy; this is
representative of Arthur's comic
work at its best, and presents
us with an iconic image of this
powerful character.*

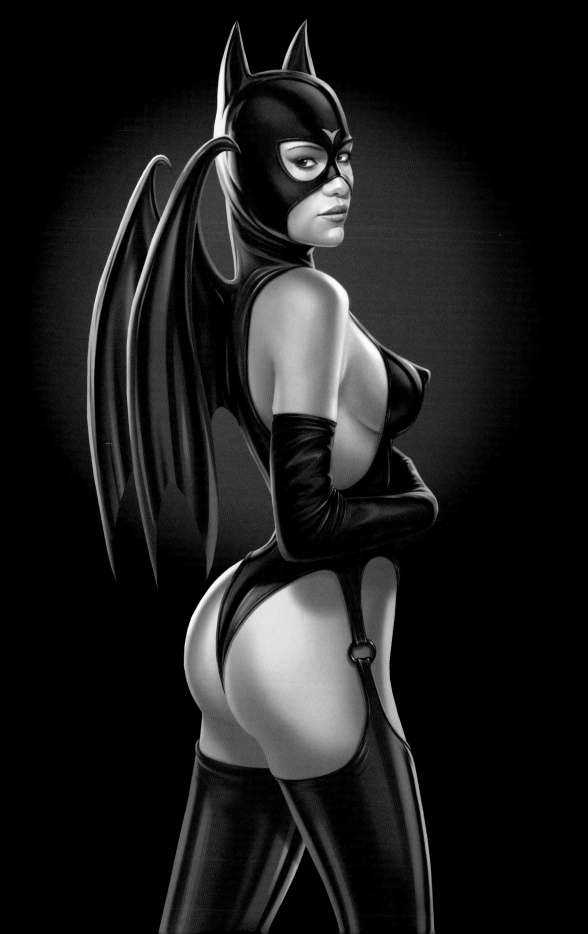

Seduction
Nestor Taylor
Client: Hot Valencia
Acrylic and airbrush

This is another image from Nestor that combines bat imagery and a sexy lady in some skimpy clothing. The rubber costume combines a fetishistic feel with the superhero outfits most of us are more familiar with. There's plenty of flesh on display and the subject stares out at the viewer, daring us to take a look.

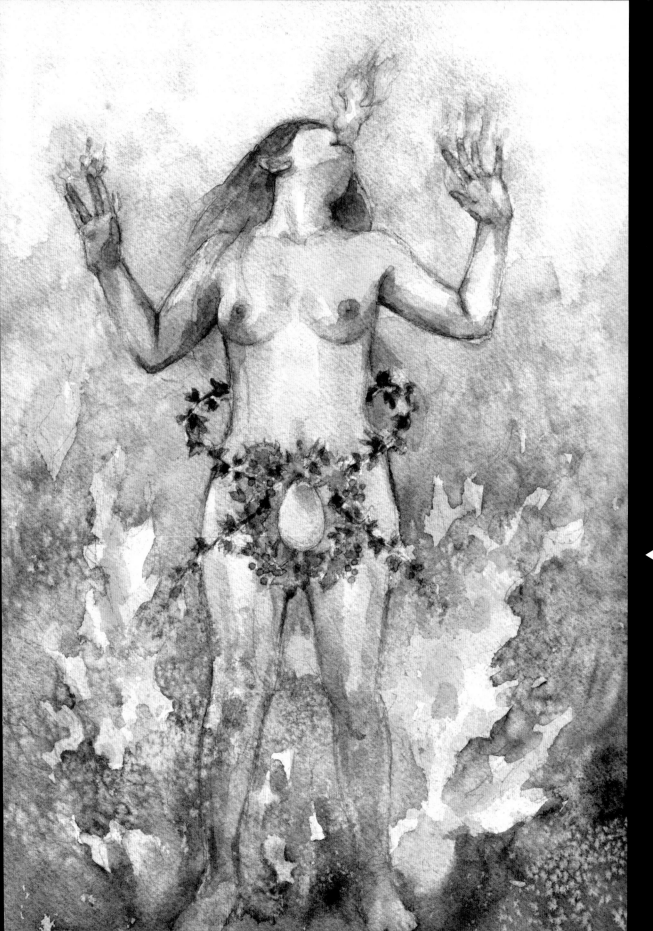

◀ **Semele**
Joanna Barnum
Portfolio piece
Graphite and watercolor
www.joannabarnum.com

In Greek mythology, Semele is one of the many lovers of Zeus. He promises to grant her anything she desires, so Semele asks to behold Zeus in all of his divine splendor. Zeus cannot break his promise, but he is heartbroken because he knows that granting this wish to the mortal Semele will destroy her. The image of Semele in flames is a metaphor for both divine and romantic ecstasy. The egg, ivy, and grape vines symbolize Dionysus, god of revelry and decadence, whom Zeus will rescue from Semele's womb.

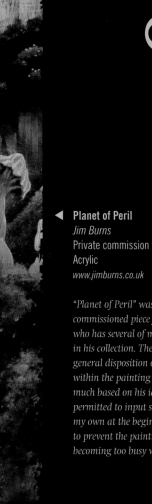

CHAPTER 6
FUTURISTIC FEMALES AND SCI-FI FOXES

◀ **Planet of Peril**
Jim Burns
Private commission
Acrylic
www.jimburns.co.uk

"Planet of Peril" was a privately commissioned piece for a friend who has several of my paintings in his collection. The title and general disposition of elements within the painting are very much based on his ideas. I was permitted to input some ideas of my own at the beginning though to prevent the painting from becoming too busy with detail!

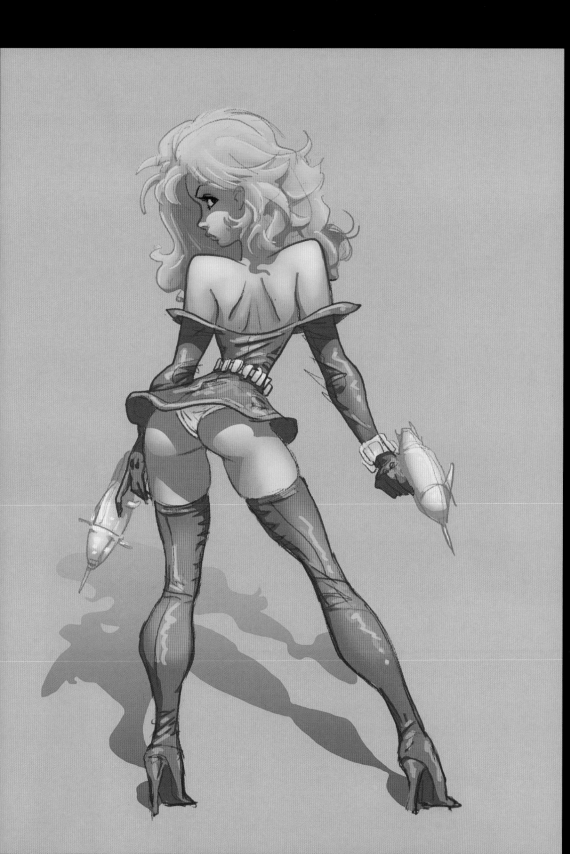

◄◄ **Flow Of Ideas**
Billy Nunez
Personal piece
Digital media: Adobe Photoshop,
Corel Painter
www.biz20.biz

*This is one of my first pieces
of work using Corel Painter.
Compositionally, this was
inspired by the work of Gustav
Klimt. I love how he combined
realistic figures with design and
pattern. I tried the same thing
in my style using my ladies,
and a lot of hair to create the
composition*

◄ **Bubblegun Babe**
Ben Tan
Colored by Ian Spendloff
Portfolio piece
Digital media: Adobe Photoshop,
Corel Painter
http://bentan.bellefree.com
www.ianspendloff.com

*The latest in chic future retro
fashion. Of course any self-
respecting space vixen outfit
would not be fully accessorized
without matching ray guns!*

▶ **Speed Racing Pin-up**
Cyril Van Der Haegen
Portfolio piece
Corel Painter
www.tegehel.org

This piece is just a simple pin-up I made to try new brushes in Painter. Actually, I like the simplicity of the design and I intend one day to create enough other pinups to make a calendar, or even a book... who knows?

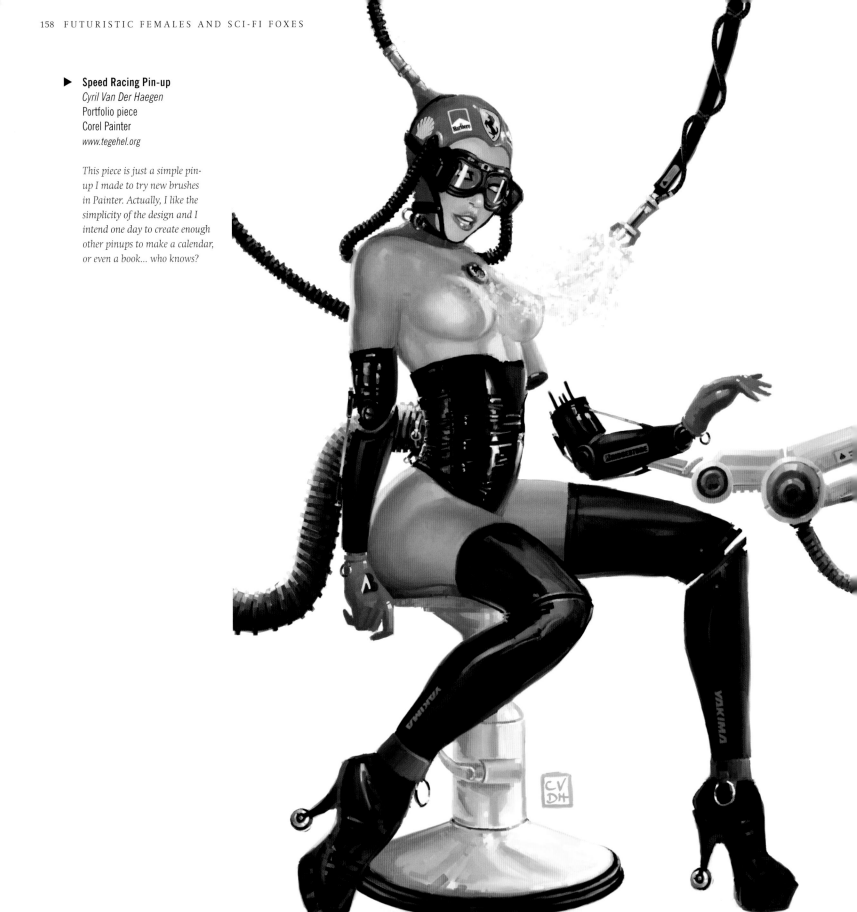

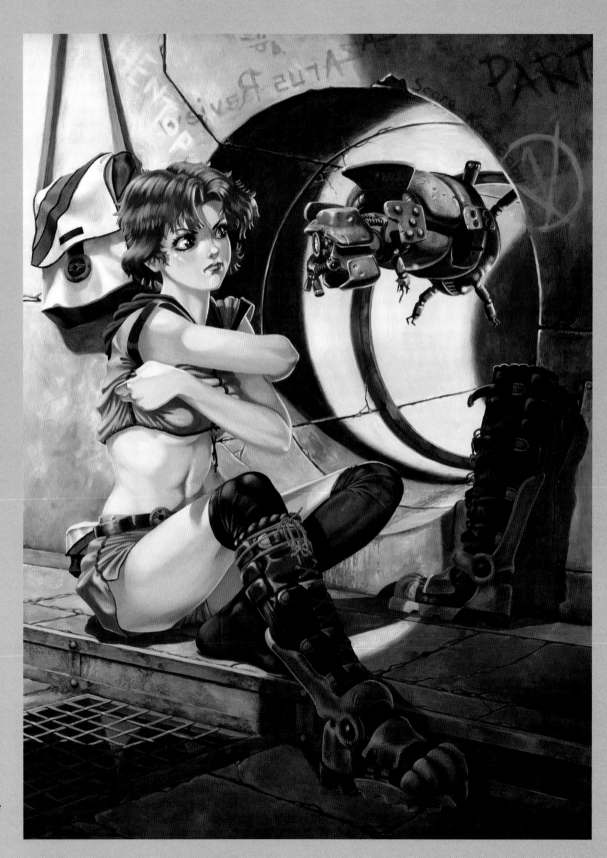

▶ **Courier X**
Andy Hepworth
Concept art for comic proposal
Client: Iain Lowson
Oil on illustration board
www.andyhepworth.com

This is a rare painting for me, as it's produced mostly with oil paints, which I rarely have time to get out of the cupboard nowadays. This was also a rare job where I had an almost free hand in design and execution. It was an opportunity to indulge myself in cute, chunky, semi-manga design.

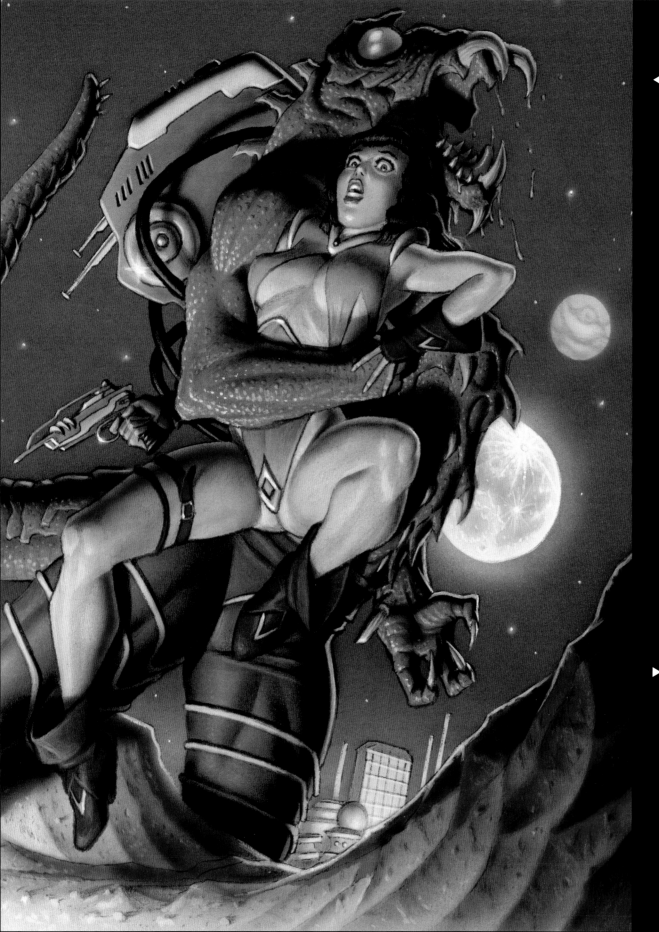

◄ **Planetnapped**
Fastner & Larson
Traditional media
www.fastnerandlarson.com

A true master of all media, Steve (Fastner) used an assortment of magic markers, Badger, Golden and Com Art acrylic airbrush paints, Verithin color pencils and Windsor Newton gouache on this painting. It first appeared as a page in the story Battlehookers of Klarn. Steve lit the scene from below for maximum B-movie ambience, and gave the girl a light blue costume to help her pop out of the composition. As if she couldn't pop out by herself!

▶ **Modern Medusa**
Robh Ruppel
Portfolio piece
Pencil and Adobe Photoshop
www.broadviewgraphics.com

Robh produces work in a variety of styles, from realistically painted creatures, environments, and women, to cleverly stylized characters that draw on fantasy and sci-fi themes. For this piece he has taken the mythical character of Medusa and given her a very modern twist.

Modern Medusa
© Robh

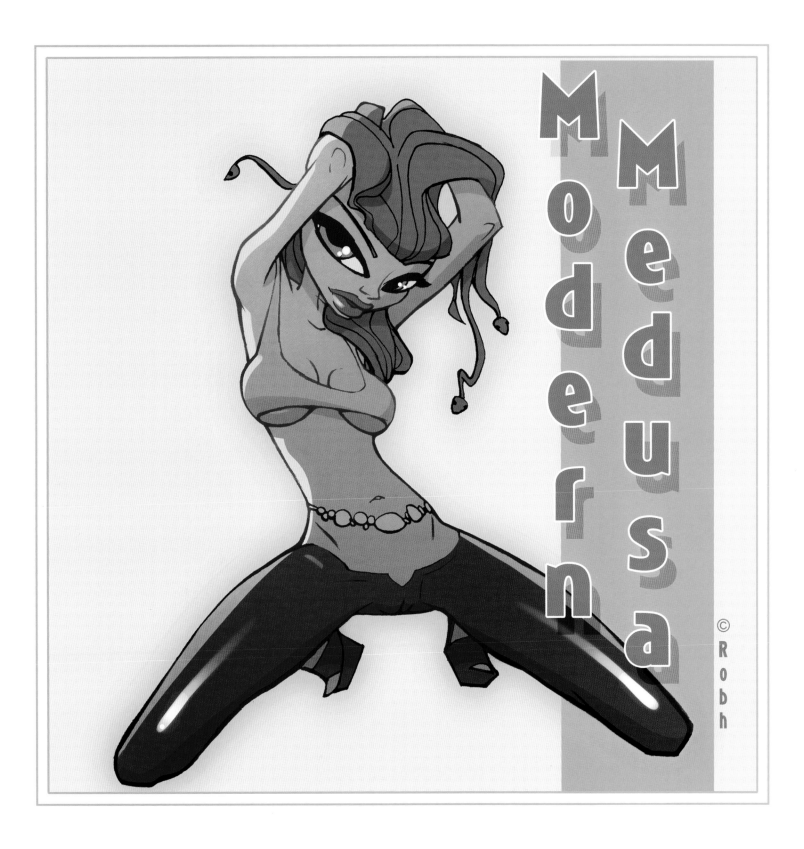

163

◄ **Jumpsuit**
Ben Tan
Portfolio piece
Digital media; Adobe Photoshop,
Corel Painter
http://bentan.bellefree.com

*In this retro-inspired piece
from Ben Tan we're offered a
curvaceous girl in a space suit
that could only have been made
for her! Her clothing provides
the skin-tight costume favored
by any self-respecting heroine,
but as Ben points out, "Pressure
suits still need to provide room
to breathe!"*

 Gazooks 3
Nic Klein
Portfolio piece
Corel Painter
www.nic-klein.com

*Nic's wonderfully entertaining
image portrays a dastardly
vixen proud of her efforts to
elude the hapless law! Cheeky
and self-knowing, she keeps us
on her side, even though we're
ignorant of her crimes! This
image is digitally executed,
yet has a traditional feel
thanks to the subdued color
scheme and homage to
traditional pin-up art.*

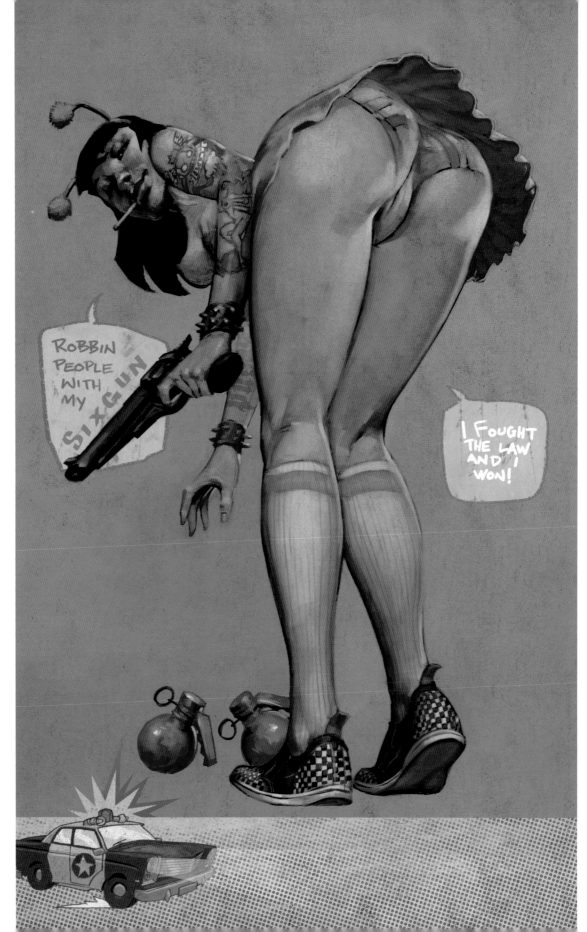

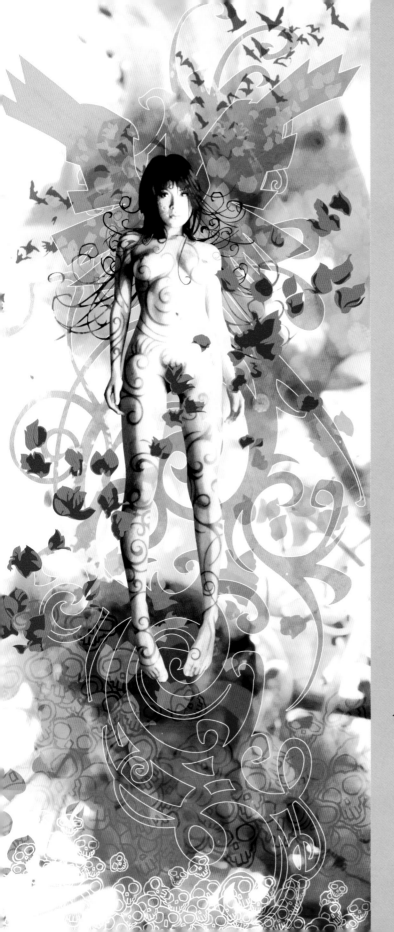

◄ **Tennyo (Heavenly Being)**
Steve Sampson
Portfolio piece
Adobe Photoshop and Illustrator
www.sampsonart.com

*Angels... I was interested to read
what other cultures had to say
on the subject. Tennin, including
the female "Tennyo", are spirits
found in Japanese Buddhism —
similar to Western angels.*

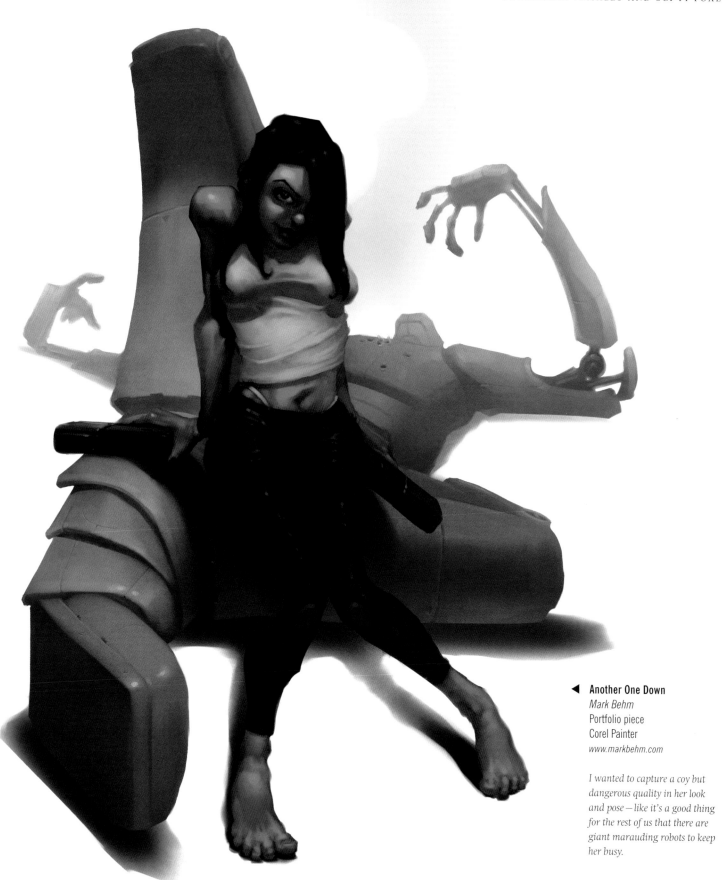

◄ **Another One Down**
Mark Behm
Portfolio piece
Corel Painter
www.markbehm.com

I wanted to capture a coy but dangerous quality in her look and pose — like it's a good thing for the rest of us that there are giant marauding robots to keep her busy.

In GOLD we trust
Vote GOLD
Vote GOLD

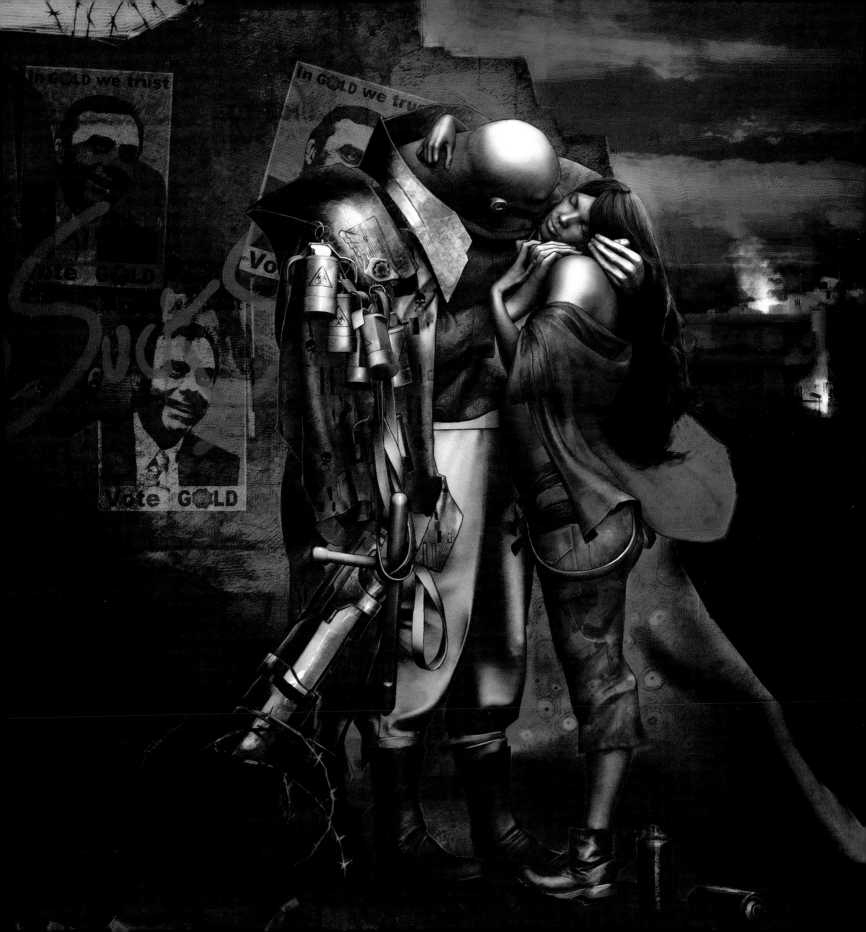

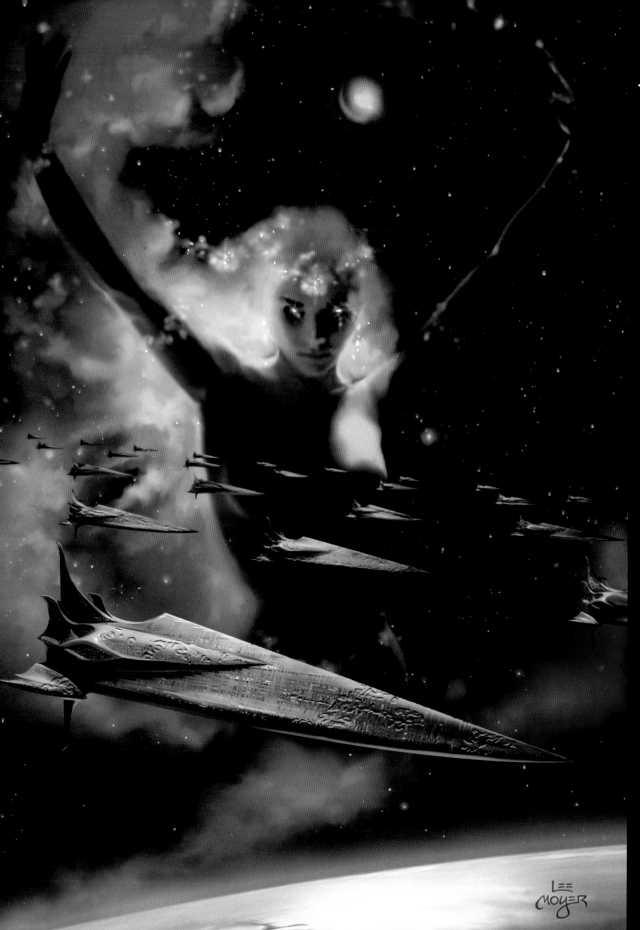

◄◄ **The Kiss**
Loic (e338) Zimmermann
Illustratio: *Imagine FX*
Digital media
www.e338.com

This is a re-interpretation of a Gustav Klimt painting. The idea was to transpose this painting into a futuristic setting. It's the story of an impossible love between an officer working for a despotic senator (Gold), and a young riot girl.

◄ **Nebula**
Lee Moyer
Portfolio piece
Pencil, Adobe Photoshop, Bryce, Corel Painter
www.leemoyer.com

This piece serves as a bridge between the 500 cards I drew for a fantasy game (Sanctum) and the vastly larger science fiction game (Star Chamber) I was about to undertake. The juxtaposition of those genres struck me as interesting.

▶ **Juicy**
Francis Hsu
Portfolio piece
Adobe Photoshop
www.iamfrancis.com

This piece started out as a doodle for an art forum. The original design was inspired by work from another artist called Francis. I've changed it since then, so it has become its own being now. I think it's awesome that as artists we always begin where someone else ends.

▶ **Durham Red: Empty Suns**
Mark Harrison
Client: 2000 AD/Rebellion
Pen, pencil, watercolor, Adobe
Photoshop, Corel Painter, Bryce
www.2000ad.org/markus/

*With this graphic novel cover
I wanted to complement what
I had intended in the comic
strip, namely a cinematic look.
To that end, I designed a "film
poster" in the style of Noriyoshi
Ohrai (who did the memorable
"Empire Strikes Back" film
poster). The use of vibrant color
helps delineate between various
elements in a stylistic way, but
requires careful thought. Much
of the central figure of Red was
"borrowed" from other paintings
I had done, which I warped to
fit, and repainted. To cement
the various elements in the final
composite, watercolor and rough
pastel filters were selectively
applied. Praise be to Photoshop!*

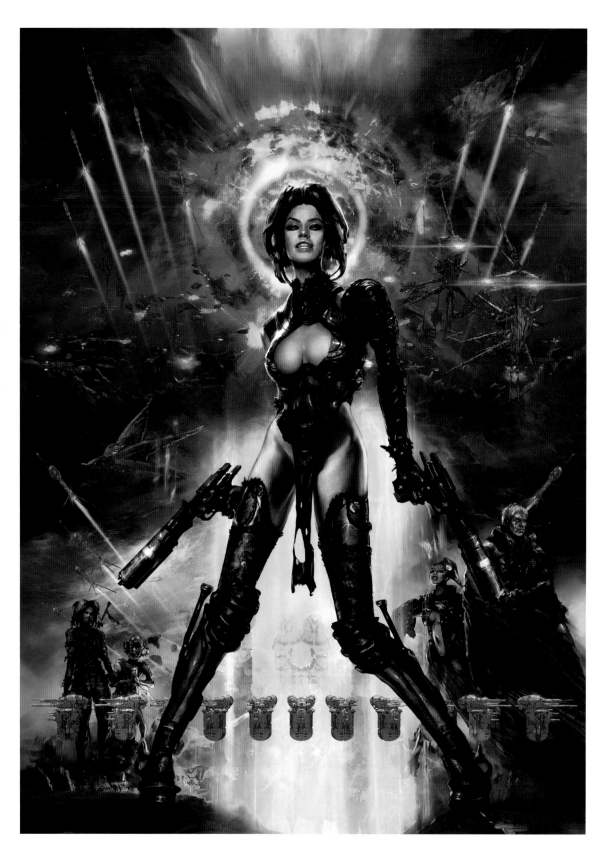

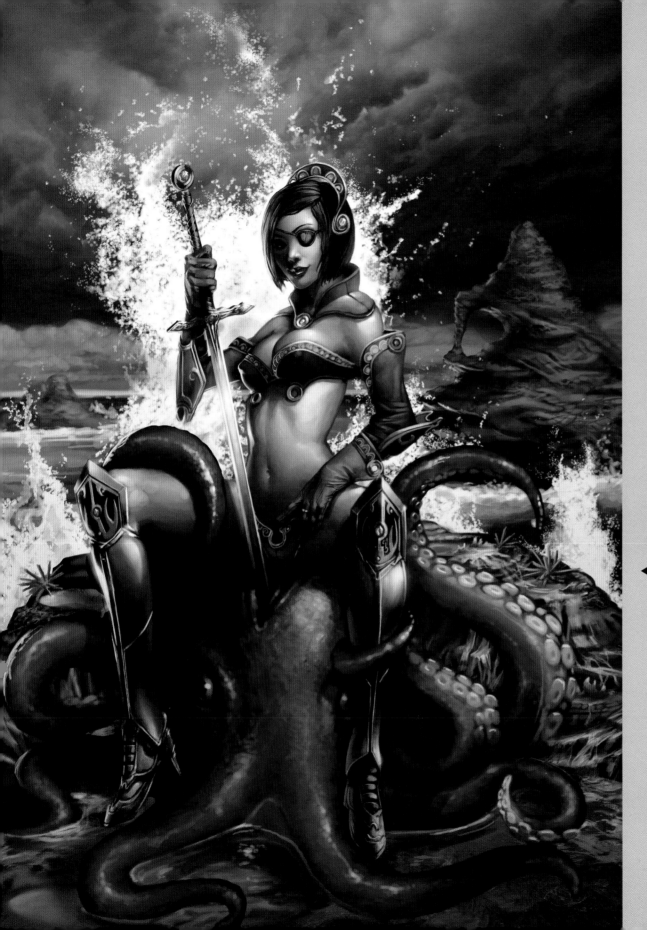

Octovagina
Peter Mohrbacher & Emily Warren
Digital media
www.vandalhigh.com

*We always heard that you need
three things to make a popular
illustration. First, you need to
feature a beautiful woman, then
you need to place her in front
of some sort of landscape, and
finally to make sure that the
illustration is predominantly
blue. If you are going to make
a painting with the express
intention of being exploitative,
it seems worthwhile going all
the way. We know sweet loving
cephalopods aren't necessarily
part of the formula, but when
you get an excuse to draw
tentacles, you just have to take it!*

▶ **Breezy**
Ben Tan
Portfolio piece
Corel Painter
http://bentan.bellefree.com

*In the privacy of space a
person can wear whatever
they want when they fly,
though impromptu stops
may be a tad... breezy!
Or perhaps it is merely
the fashion of the day?*

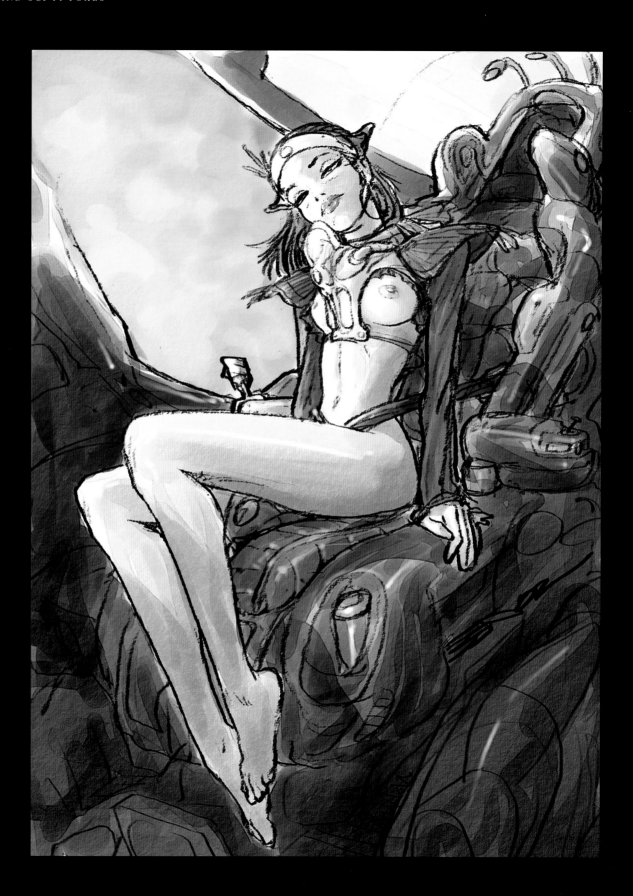

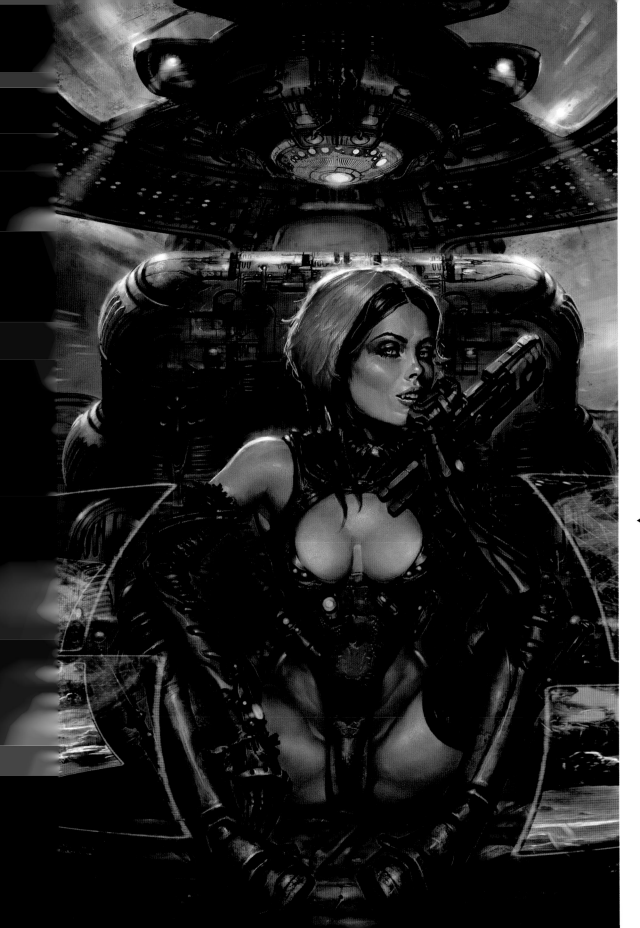

Durham Red: Black Dawn
Mark Harrison
Client: Black Flame/Rebellion
Pencil, watercolor, Adobe
Photoshop, Corel Painter, Bryce
www.2000ad.org/markus/

*Having illustrated the mutant
vampire bounty hunter "Durham
Red" for over 13 years in the comic
2000 AD, I felt I had an informed
perspective on her character
when illustrating the novels. She
wouldn't sit demurely in her
star ship; she'd sit poised, like a
mantrap. Enticing and deadly, her
confidence is intimidating. She's in
control, and the cocked blaster she
cradles reinforces that. Too much
for the publisher however, who
censored the final image. Pussies!
Red herself is scanned pencil and
watercolor, composited into a
Bryce modelled cockpit that was
heavily repainted.*

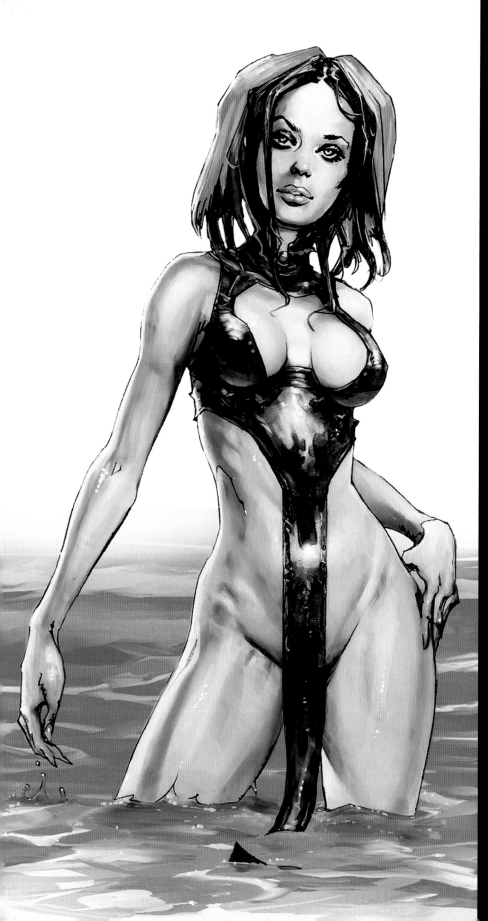

◀ **Red Sea**
Mark Harrison
Client: A fan
Pencil, watercolor, Corel Painter
http://www.2000ad.org/markus/

*A while back a fan wrote to me
requesting a pencil sketch of
Durham Red. The sketch turned
out better than expected so I
kept a scan of the image. Later,
I was looking for art to practise
on with the new Corel Painter
software I had bought. I used
the sketch and this is the result.
Where do mutant vampires
go on holiday? To the shores of
the Red Sea of Blood of course!
It's clean and simple, but has
significance for me as it was a
turning point from traditional
art towards the exciting
possibilities of digital painting.*

▶ **Voidslime**
Jim Murray
Illustration: *Magic: The Gathering*
Acrylic on illustration board
www.jimmurrayart.com

*This dynamic piece from Jim
started out with a pretty vague
brief from his client: "I think
the brief was something like 'a
female mage in mid spell cast,
being hit by a coiling rope of
ickiness, a mixture of kelp, snot,
vine and squid tentacles…" I like
it when they're specific like that!"*

Time's Illusion

Martin Abel

Commission: *Picture Premium*
magazine
Digital media
www.martinabel.com

*The symbolism here suggests
the title. Yin and Yang and the
clock face imagery all add up to
a mysterious metaphor, but that
takes second place to the sultry
girl around which it all revolves.*

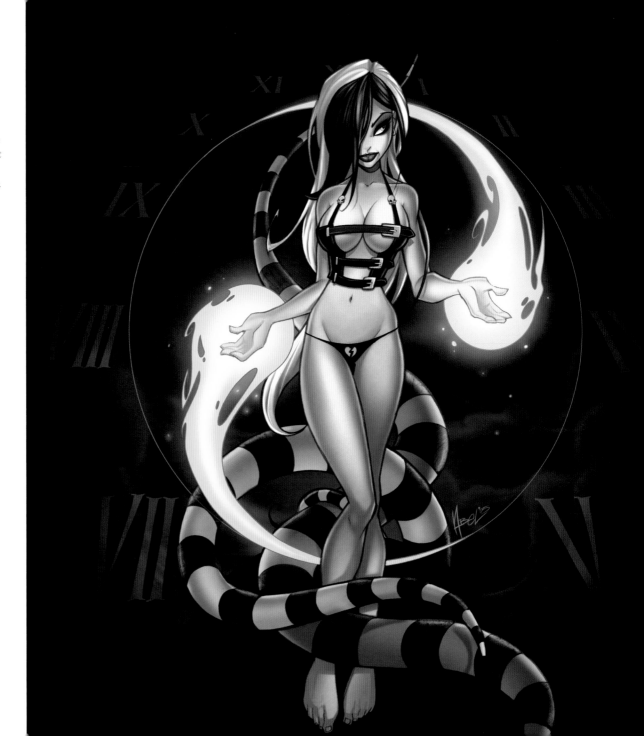

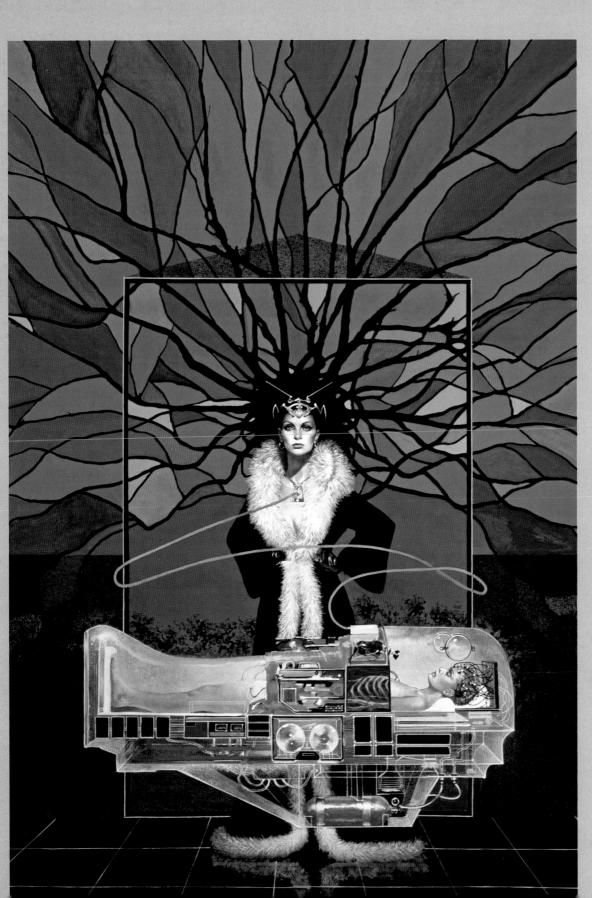

◀ **This Year's Model**
Don Maitz
Book cover: *Electric Forest*
Daw Books
Acrylic
www.paravia.com/DonMaitz

An acrylic painting featuring an android enlightened with the consciousness of the woman in the stasis tank. The background elements were made by blowing wet acrylics with a straw.

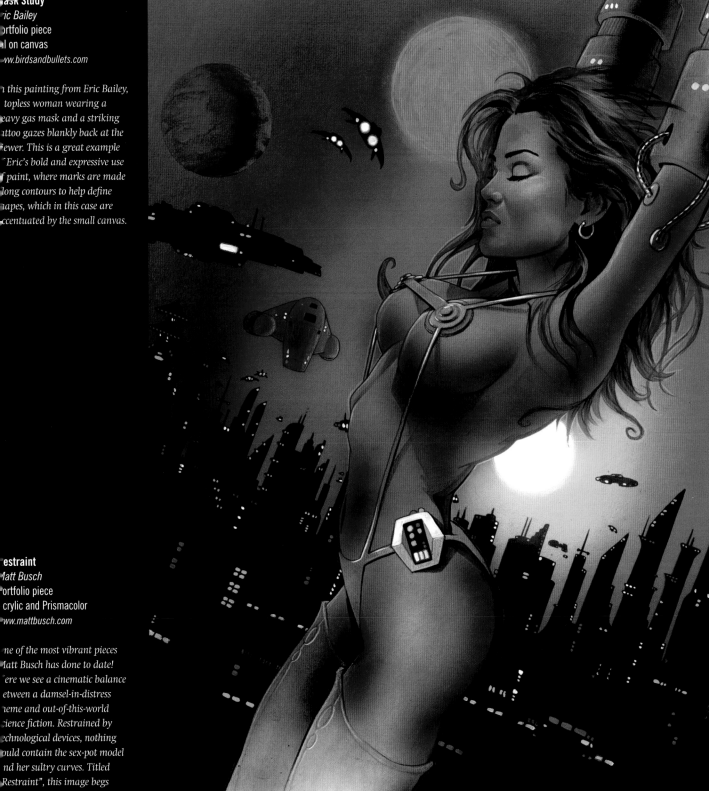

ask Study

ic Bailey
ortfolio piece
l on canvas
ww.birdsandbullets.com

*n this painting from Eric Bailey,
 topless woman wearing a
eavy gas mask and a striking
attoo gazes blankly back at the
ewer. This is a great example
 Eric's bold and expressive use
f paint, where marks are made
long contours to help define
apes, which in this case are
ccentuated by the small canvas.*

estraint

Matt Busch
ortfolio piece
crylic and Prismacolor
ww.mattbusch.com

*ne of the most vibrant pieces
Matt Busch has done to date!
ere we see a cinematic balance
etween a damsel-in-distress
heme and out-of-this-world
cience fiction. Restrained by
echnological devices, nothing
ould contain the sex-pot model
nd her sultry curves. Titled
Restraint", this image begs*

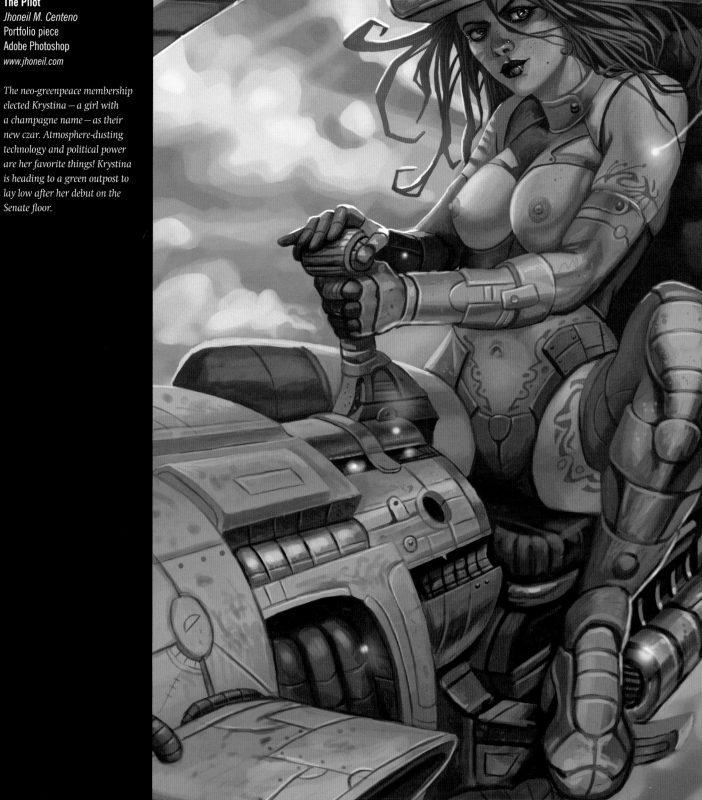

The Pilot
Jhoneil M. Centeno
Portfolio piece
Adobe Photoshop
www.jhoneil.com

The neo-greenpeace membership
elected Krystina — a girl with
a champagne name — as their
new czar. Atmosphere-dusting
technology and political power
are her favorite things! Krystina
is heading to a green outpost to
lay low after her debut on the
Senate floor.

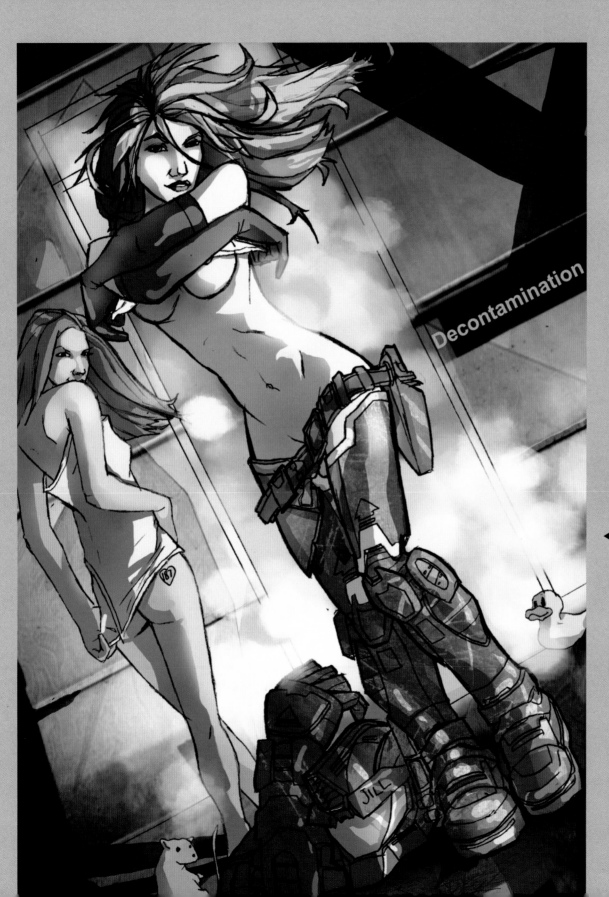

◀ **Decontamination**
David Cousens
Portfolio piece
Pencils and Adobe Photoshop
www.CoolSurface.com

Not all fantasy art is based on
the height of the action, and for
every barbarian, space heroine
or employee of heavy industry,
there's always going to be a
time when they need to wind
down and get cleaned up. Here's
David's own interpretation
of his futuristic shower scene:
"Interstellar Mining Corporation
regulation #187/2707-S: Upon
the cessation of operations, all
workers are required to report
to the shower block immediately
for thorough decontamination.
Rubber duck is optional."

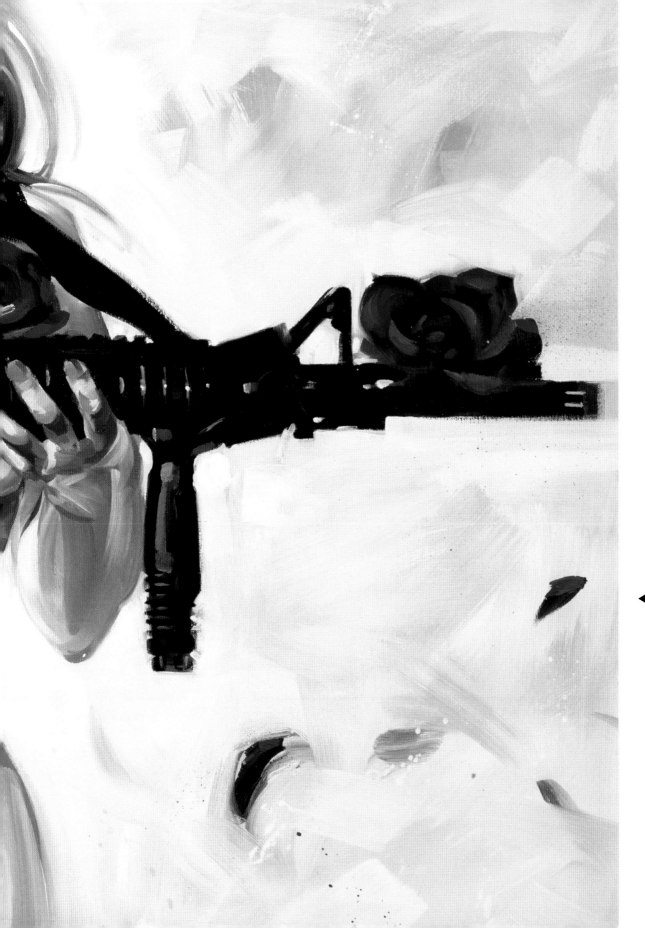

◀ **Heavy**
Eric Bailey
Portfolio piece
Oil on canvas
www.birdsandbullets.com

In this simple study of a naked
woman and an M16 Eric
contrasts the delicate beauty of
the figure and the roses against
the hard lines of the assault rifle.
The contrast is further enforced
by the use of colour, with the
strong black silhouette of the
gun placed against the pale
pinks that make up the rest of
the canvas. Strung along the
top of the gun are three blood
red roses, some of whose petals
flutter helplessly off canvas.

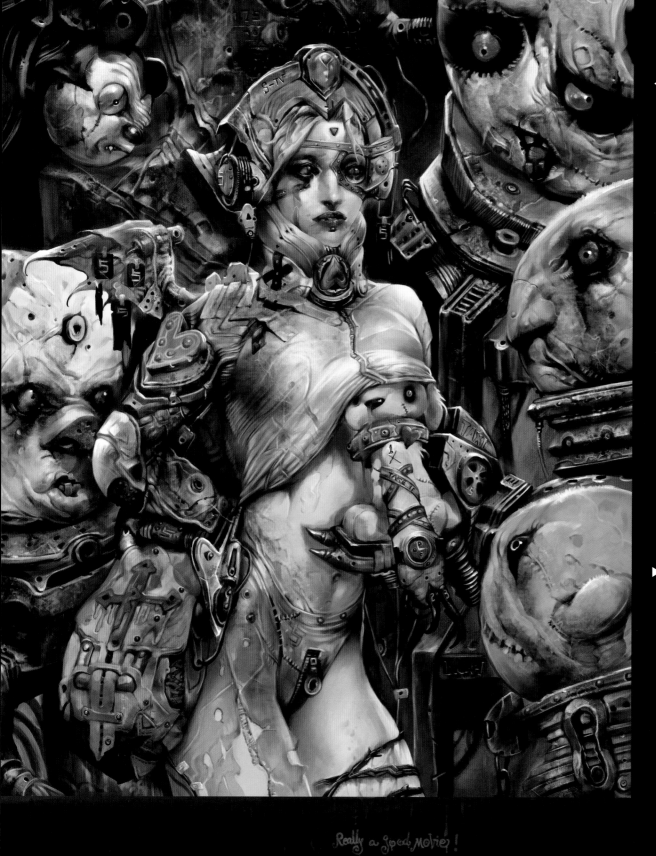

Really a Good Movie !

◄ **A Movie About Rabbit**
Kuang Hong
Portfolio piece
Digital media: Adobe Photoshop
and Corel Painter
www.zemotion.net

The detail the artist has
incorporated into this image
has become a staple of his work.
Truly stunning attention to color,
composition, and layout have
produced a picture of intricacy
and depth, with a subtle humor
that reveals his personality, and
draws the viewer in.

▶ **DAM5EL IN DI5TRE55**
Matt Busch
Portfolio piece
Acrylic and Prismacolor
www.mattbusch.com

Artist Matt Busch set this epic
beauty in an other-worldly,
cybernetic locale, with a classic
damsel in distress mood. Busch
had worked previously with
model Shannon for STUN
magazine and claims; "I love
the classic B-Movie damsel in
distress thing, but I wanted to
see it in a genre we're not used
to. Everything about this piece
was experimental. Even the color
harmony is kind of crazy, and
off the beaten path for my
palette." A path Busch should
take more often, perhaps...?

Ivoria Lamenting
Kino Siablabba
Portfolio piece
Digital media
www. homepage.mac.com/kinoo/
PhotoAlbum4.html

The soothing gentle blue of this
image contrasts with the sadness
suggested by the title. Why is
Ivoria lamenting, and what is
her loss? The open composition
and use of negative space above
the character are other examples
of Kino's strong design sense.

▶ **Obsession**
Francis Tsai
Game illustration
Digital media
www.teamgt.com

"Obsession" is another Darkwatch
video game marketing illustration.
The studio I worked for at the time
was very art-centric, and went
to great lengths to promote the
artwork and concept design of the
games in various magazines and
online news sites.

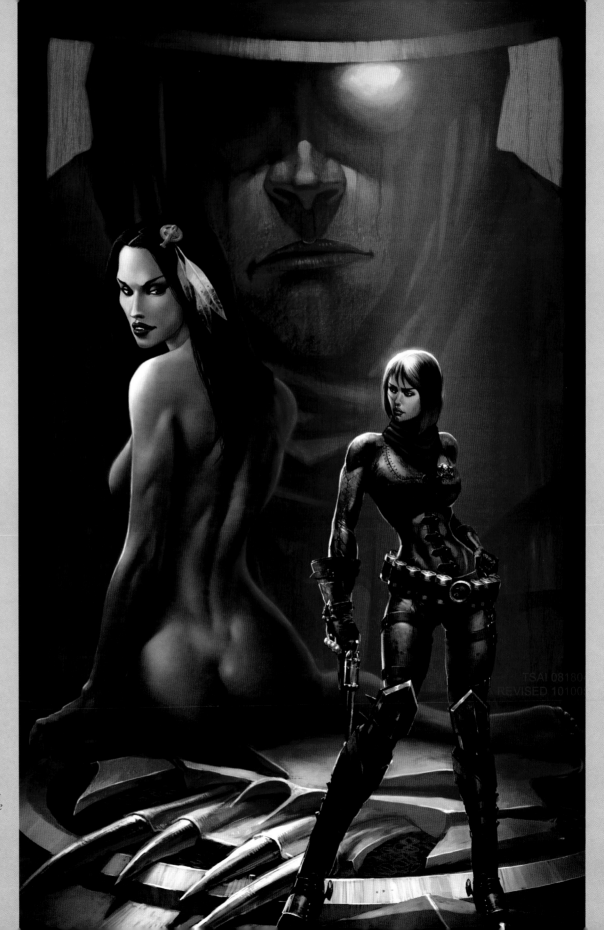

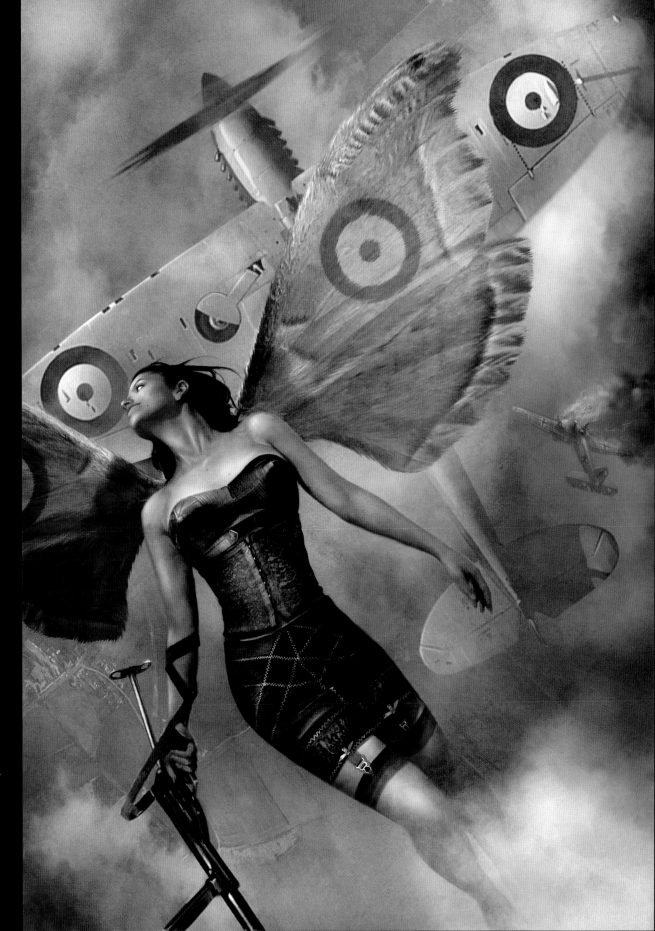

◀ **Flight**
Hoang Nguyen
Illustration: *Imagine FX*
Adobe Photoshop
www.liquidbrush.com

Hoang is an artist working in the games industry, but produced "Flight" for a tutorial in Imagine FX magazine. His simple composition places the emphasis on the beauty of the girl. Her delicate sensuality contrasts with the dark mass and strong lines of the flying hat, and the bold tattoo on her right shoulder.

▶ **Victory Gal Tranquility**
Glen Angus
Portfolio piece
Adobe Photoshop
www.gangus.net

This painting was done as part of my "Victory Gals" body of work. It is probably one of my best examples of combining a peaceful atmosphere within the context of war. The "Victory Gal" concept itself was born of the thought of the nose art on planes taking the angelic form of an actual protector or ward for the pilot or pilots. It is a subject matter that I truly love depicting, because it offers the ability to take pin-up subjects and combine them with my love of aviation. I also get to create my own lingerie designs based on inspirational pieces from those days. This piece is also noted to have won the 2007 Digital Art CGOVERDRIVE Gold Award.

MARTIN ABEL
www.martinabel.com
martin@martinabel.com
Twenty Four *p79*
Roswell High *p84*
Time's Illusion *p176*

GLEN ANGUS
www.gangus.net
Ophelia *p66*
Victory Gal: Angel of Death p127
Victory Gal: Spitfire *p189*

DAREN BADER
www.darenbader.com
daren@darenbader.com
The Harpy *p98*

ERIC BAILEY
www.birdsandbullets.com
eric@birdsandbullets.com
Angel Study *p124*
Mask Study *p178*
Heavy *p182*

JOANNA BARNUM
www.joannabarnum.com
joanna@joannabarnum.com
Semele *p153*

ANDREW BAWIDAMANN
www.bawidamann.com
andrew@bawidamann.com
MG42 Madchen *p29*

MARK BEHM
www.markbehm.com
markbehm@markbehm.com
Another One Down *p165*

JOHN BLUMEN
www.portfolios.com/johnblumen
jjblumen@aol.com
Lucy *p99*

CHRISTIAN BRAVERY
www.leadinglightdesign.com
studio@leadinglightdesign.com
Willing Victim *p143*

SIMON DOMINIC BREWER
www.painterly.co.uk
simon@painterly.co.uk
The Green Man *p17*

BROM
www.bromart.com
morbx@comcast.net
Angel *p55*

JIM BURNS
www.jimburns.co.uk
jim_burns@blueyonder.co.uk
Sirpa, of the Guild of Vammatar
p27
The Dryad of the Oaks *p96*
Planet of Peril *p154*

MATT BUSCH
www.mattbusch.com
matt@mattbusch.com
Statuesque *p90*
Sensual Summoning *p94*
Restraint *p179*
DAM5EL IN DI5TRE55 *p185*

JHONEIL M. CENTENO
www.jhoneil.com
jhoneil@jhoneil.com
The Pilot *p180*

JASON CHAN
www.jasonchanart.com
jason@jasonchanart.com
Red Riding Hood *p45*

DAVID COUSENS
www.coolsurface.com
david@coolsurface.com
Djinn *p78*
Decontamination *p181*

RAUL CRUZ
www.racrufi.com
raul@racrufi.com
Agua de Jade *p59*

ALAN DANIELS
www.heavenlyhusseys.com
www.fetish-pinups.com
alan@heavenlyhussys.com
Devotional Aspiration *p42*
Recline *p88*
Curator *p93*

SACHA (ANGEL) DIENER
www.angel3d.ch
angel@angel3d.ch
Dark Romance *p57*
Divided Heart *p101*

JONNY DUDDLE
www.duddlebug.co.uk
jonny@duddlebug.co.uk
The Siren *p8*

CRAIG ELLIOT
www.craigelliotgallery.com
craig@craigelliotgallery.com
Flower Expanse *p128*
Vampiresses Fishing *p146*

KAREEM ETTOUNEY
www.kareemettouney.com
hello@kareemettouney.com
Angels *p107*

FASTNER & LARSON
www.fastnerandlarson.com
mail@fastnerandlarson.com
Spangled 'n Tangled *p61*
Midnight Tea *p62*
Planetnapped *p160*

ALY FELL
www.darkrising.co.uk
alyfell@darkrising.co.uk
Boing! *p11*
The Black Queen *p21*
The Chalice *p54*
CHARGE! *p92*

TOM FLEMING
www.flemart.com
flemart@bellsouth.net
Mermaiden *p114*
Spring *p126*
Soul Harvest *p135*

RIC FRANE
www.ricfrane.com
ric@ricfrane.com
Golden Dragon *p40*
Ssss... *p46*
Nosferatu *p72*

CYRIL VAN DER HAEGEN
www.tegehel.org
tegehel@cox.net
Styx *p56*
Sylvan Spirit *p91*
Speed-Racing Pinup *p158*

MARK HARRISON
sarah.markus@blueyonder.co.uk
www.2000ad.org/markus

Dragon Girl *p65*
Durham Red: Empty Suns *p170*
Durham Red: Black Dawn *p173*
Red Sea *p174*

ANDY HEPWORTH
www.andyhepworth.com
hepworthandrew@aol.com
Elsine *p48*
Canaltown Princess *p60*
Holly Temptation *p108*
Courier X *p159*

STEPHEN HICKMAN
www.stephenhickman.com
shickman@stephenhickman.com
The Lemurian Princess *p30*
The Sea of Vaynu *p41*

JESSICA HOOK
www.jessicahook.com
jessica@jessicahook.com
Mermaid *p112*

KUANG HONG
www.zemotion.net
noah@zemotion.net
Witchery *p81*
Melody of Spring *p102*
A Movie about Rabbit *p184*

ALEX HORLEY
www.alexhorley.com
horley@iol.it
Messalina *p14*
Maxine *p34*
Red Stacy *p35*
Stacy & Her Pumpkin *p73*

FRANCIS HSU
www.iamfrancis.com
ultrahsu@gmail.com
Juicy *p169*

MATT HUGHES
www.matthughesart.com
matthughesart@yahoo.com
Becoming *p75*
Zpheru's Gate *p100*

BJÖRN HURRI
www.bjornhurri.com
bjornhurri@hotmail.com
Siri—The Princess *p68*
The Empress *p95*

ANDREW (ANDROID) JONES
www.androidjones.com
ajones@spectrum.net
The 3 Muses *p82*
Fire Fight Fuck *p134*

PATRICK J JONES
www.pjartworks.com
deanjo@pjartworks.com
Masquerade *p50*
Seraph *p118*
Vampyre Planet *p138*

NIC KLEIN
www.nic-klein.com
me@nic-klein.com
Gazooks 3 *p163*

STEPH LABERIS
www.flyingclam.com
stephlaberis@gmail.com
Evening Dip *p192*

SCOTT LEWIS
www.lewisart.com
scott@lewisart.com
Leopard Girl *p16*

HENNING LUDVINGSEN
www.henningludvigsen.com
henlu@online.no
Goh Cephal *p80*
Wall *p130*

DON MAITZ
www.paravia.com/donmaitz
donmaitz@paravia.com
Conjure Maitz *p71*
The Oracle *p86*
This Year's Model *p177*

**MALACHAI MALONEY
(LIQUIDWERX)**
www.liquidwerx.com
malachi@liquidwerx.com
Blackjack Betty *p28*
Soul Drinker *p74*

TONY MAURO
www.darkdayproductions.com
tmauro@earthlink.net
The Tank *p38*
Red Ribbons *p85*
The Light *p119*
O'lovely fairy *p120*

ISMAEL (IZZY) MEDRANO
www.mercilessdesign.com
cannibalcandy@gmail.com
Chloe *p36*

**PETER MORBACHER AND
EMILY WARREN**
www.vandalhigh.com
bugmeyer@gmail.com
Octovagina *p171*

LEE MOYER
www.leemoyer.com
lee@leemoyer.com
The Ebon Mirror *p25*
Port Royale *p70*
Nebula *p168*

JIM MURRAY
www.jimmurrayart.com
info@jimmurrayart.com
Radha, Heir to Keld *p13*
Voidslime *p175*

VINCE NATALE
www.vincenatale.com
vince@vincenatale.com
Raven *p39*
Love Lies Dying *p142*

MARK NELSON
www.grazingdinosaurpress.com
gdpmark@chorus.net
AG Thought *p49*
E2 Metis *p122*
RR Morganna *p149*

HOANG NGUYEN
www.liquidbrush.com
Hoang@liquidbrush.com
Flight *p188*

BILLY NUNEZ
www.biz20.biz
biz20ymf@gmail.com
Flow Of Ideas *p156*

BEN OLSON
www.sketchthing.com
sketchthing@gmail.com
Asylum of Horrors *p32*

KIP OMOLADE
www.kipomolade.com
kip@kipomolade.com

Metamorphosis *p58*

GLEN ORBIK
www.orbikart.com
glenandlaurel@earthlink.net
Wizard's Champion *p23*

R K POST
www.rkpost.net
postrk@aol.com
Broken World *p20*
Tangents *p64*
Indigestion *p145*

TARIQ RAHEEM
www.tariqart.com
tariq12.raheem@gmail.com
Raven *p15*
Rebecca Fantasy *p31*
Ina's Angel *p106*

PATRICK REILLY
http://preilly.deviantart.com/gallery
reilly1138@msn.com
Demona *p136*

NATASCHA ROEOESLI
www.tascha.ch
n@tascha.ch
The Wax-dragon *p44*
The Soul Collector *p139*

MARK E. ROGERS
www.merogers.com
merogers@delanet.com
Bode Babe *p47*

ROBH RUPPEL
www.broadviewgraphics.com
robhrr@yahoo.com
Modern Medusa *p161*

STEVE SAMPSON
www.sampsonart.com
sampson_art@zen.co.uk
O Abate (The Slaughter) *p18*
Anjo Do Mal (Dark Angel) *p115*
Tennyo (Heavenly Being) *p164*

KINO SCIALABBA
http://homepage.mac.com/kinoo/
PhotoAlbum4.html
kinoo@mac.com
Hope 13 *p150*
Ivoria Lamenting *p186*

YUKO SHIMIZU
www.yukoart.com
yuko@yukoart.com
Panda Girl: The First
Asian-American Superheroine *p26*

LORENZO SPERLONGA
www.lorenzosperlonga.com
spiderello@aol.com
Ivy *p43*
Silk Blossom *p52*
Absynthe *p109*
White Angel *p121*

CHRIS SPOLLEN
www.spollen.com
cjspollen@aol.com
Beach Girl *p53*
Buoy Four *p140*

ARTHUR SUYDAM
www.arthursuydam.com
nyccreativegroup@earthlink.net
The Albatrose *p63*
Phoenix *p151*

BEN TAN
http://bentan.bellefree.com
bentan@bellefree.com
Bubblegun Babe *p157*
Jumpsuit *p162*
Breezy *p172*

NESTOR TAYLOR
nestortaylor@hotmail.com
Blue Dream *p148*
Seduction *p152*

LES TOIL
www.toilgirls.com
lestoil@comcast.net
Angelica *p125*

FRANCIS TSAI
www.teamgt.com
tsai@teamgt.com
Duel *p24*
Obsession *p187*

DANIELA UHLIG
www.du-artwork.de
www.lolita-art.deviantart.com
danielauhlig@du-artwork.de
Art Nouveau II *p110*
Art Nouveau III *p111*

Queen of Hearts *p137*

CHRISTOPHE VACHER
www.vacher.com
christophe.vacher@excite.com
Fairy *p104*
Spirit Rising *p105*
Sacred Hour II *p123*

SVETLIN VELINOV
www.velinov.com
svetlin@velinov.com
The Dragon Princess *p22*

JOHANN DE VENECIA
Dreamcatcher Prostasia *p87*
Lance and Gwen *p116*

SHELLY WAN
shellywan.blogspot.com
shellyminwan@yahoo.com
Spring *p117*

CHAD MICHAEL WARD
www.digitalapocalypse.com
revapocalypse@yahoo.com
Saint Amie *p67*

MATT WILSON
www.mattwilsonart.com
mw@mattwilsonart.com
Cross *p33*
Wraith Queen *p76*
Chains *p132*
Lady Demon *p133*

ZHUZHU
http://zhuzhu.deviantart.com
www.artwanted.com/zhuzhu
Zhuhaibo1220@163.com
Toy *p51*

LOIC (E338) ZIMMERMANN
www.e338.com
zimmermann@club-internet.fr
Death and its Brides *p144*
The Kiss *p166*

Acknowledgments

No book is produced in isolation, and our main thanks must go to the artists who pulled out all the stops to be represented here, artists whose imagination, thankfully, knows no bounds. Of course, thanks must also go to our respective partners and soul mates—Rosie and Jane—who put up with our late hours, spoilt weekends and grumpy moods! This book is for you as well.

Glen Angus 1970 - 2007

With enormous sadness we would like to pay tribute to Glen Angus who sadly passed away in July 2007, while this book was in preparation.

Glen's "Victory Gal" series was—and is—inspiring to many who followed his work through online communities such as Concept Art and CGSociety. We are fortunate to be able to show examples of that series here, and would like to pass on our deepest affection to his family and friends.

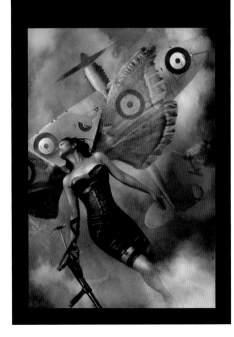

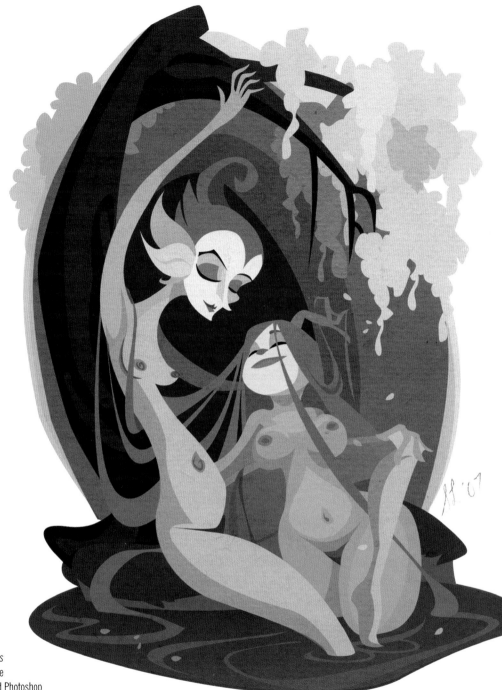

▶ **Evening Dip**
Steph Laberis
Personal piece
Illustrator and Photoshop
www.flyingclam.com

In this affectionate picture, a sultry dryad visits with her favorite water nymph. The sensual curves of women have always been inspiring to Steph and she finds that vector art lends itself well to expressing those curves. "Toss in some flower petals and hey, what can I say, I'm a romantic!"